CLASSIC BRITISH
BIKES

Andrew Kemp
and Mirco De Cet

ABBEYDALE PRESS

This edition published in 1997 by
ABBEYDALE PRESS
An imprint of Bookmart Ltd
Desford Road, Enderby,
Leicestershire LE9 5AD
England

Copyright © Bookmart 1997

ISBN 1–86147–005–3

Reprinted 1998

Exclusive to Chapters in Canada

Printed in Spain

Contents

Introduction 4

The Pioneers 1900-1920 5

Introduction 6
Humber Trike 10
Matchless................................12
Triumph 3hp 14
P&M 16
Singer 18
Norton 3½hp............................20
Wilkinson TMC 22
Ariel 3½hp 24
Bat No. 2................................26
BSA 3½hp................................28
Zenith Gradua 30
Rudge Multi 32
Triumph 3½hp...........................34
Lea-Francis 36
Royal Enfield V-twin 38
Scott 3¾ Two Speed.....................40
Clyno 42
Douglas 2¾hp 44
Wooler....................................46

Vintage Days 1920-1940.................49

Introduction 50
ABC 54
Levis Popular............................56
Norton 16H..............................58
Velocette Two-stroke 60
Triumph Ricardo 62

BSA Round Tank..........................64
James V-twin 66
Brough Superior SS100 68
Ner-a-car.................................70
Cotton TT 72
Sunbeam Model 90.....................74
Velocette KTT 76
Norton CS1 78
Scott Squirrel 80
Matchless Silver Hawk 82
Excelsior Manxman 84
Norton International 86
Vincent Rapide 88
Triumph Speed Twin 5T................90
BSA Gold Star 92
Rudge Ulster 94

The Classic Era 1940-1960 97

Introduction 98
BSA M20 102
Excelsior Welbike 104
AJS 7R..................................106
Triumph GP & Trophy 108
Vincent Rapide 110
Velocette KTT 112
LE Velocette 114
BSA Bantam 116
Norton Model 18 & ES2..............118
BSA A10 Golden Flash 120
Royal Enfield Bullet 122
Sunbeam S8 124
Vincent Black Prince 126

Ariel Square Four 128
Douglas Dragonfly.......................130
Norton Dominator 132
Velocette MSS............................134
Norton International 136
BSA Gold Star 138
Triumph Tiger Cub 140
Panther M120 142

Endings and Beginnings 1960-1991 ..145

Introduction 146
BSA C15T................................150
Ariel Leader 152
Greeves Sports Twin 154
Royal Enfield Constellation 156
Norton 500 Manx 158
BSA A65 160
Velocette Thruxton 162
BSA Rocket 3 164
Triumph T120 Bonneville.............166
Norton Commando (Fastback) 168
Norton P11 170
Norton Commando (Roadster).....172
Triumph Trident 174
Rickman Enfield Interceptor.........176
Silk 700.................................178
Triumph T140 Bonneville.............180
Hesketh Vampire.......................182
Norton Wankel Rotary 184
Triumph Trident 186
Triumph T595 Daytona 188
Triumph Thunderbird 190

Introduction

The motorcycle is little over one hundred years old. At the start of the 20th century it resembled a spindly motorised bicycle whose large but often unreliable engine offered a performance little better than a modern moped. By the end of the century, it had developed into a sophisticated and comfortable superbike, in some cases capable of sustaining speeds in excess of 150mph for hours on end.

For well over 50 years, British bikes helped to force the pace of technological change, and for several decades could honestly claim to be the best in the world. British-built machines set speed records, won races and endurance trials, carried out seemingly impossible stunts – and carried their owners to work, day in, day out.

They were the favoured mounts of princes, film stars, industrialists, soldiers – and the ordinary working man and woman. They provided their owners with entertainment and freedom, kept the wheels of commerce turning, and played a major part in both world wars as well as many lesser conflicts. British motorcycle factories exported to half the globe – and the cousins of the machines that won races in Europe could be found earning their keep in rural communities across a British Empire that spanned almost every continent.

And then it all went wrong. In part the victim of increasing affluence, in part of mismanagement and shortsightedness, the British motorbike industry collapsed. In little more than 20 years it went from being the pride of the world to a half-forgotten footnote that owed its very existence to the dedication of a small band of enthusiasts.

Even so, the names of the great marques lived on: names such as BSA, Matchless, Norton, Sunbeam, and, above all, Triumph – a name which has been proudly reborn to take on the best in the world, winning sales and performance records alike, and well able to look forward to the next century.

Classic British Bikes tells the story of the machines for which the label 'Made in England' was a badge of pride. Featuring detailed historical analyses of almost one hundred machines, it chronicles the technical innovation, engineering expertise and ingenuity that for decades made the industry a world leader, as well as the numerous efforts to restore it to its former glory.

A century of progress has taken the motorcycle from its bicycle origins (left) to become a sophisticated high-performance machine (below). The history of the machines produced by the British motor cycle industry illustrates every step of that process.

The Pioneers

1900–1920

Humber Trike ✪ Matchless ✪ Triumph 3hp ✪ P&M

Singer ✪ Norton 3½hp ✪ Wilkinson TMC ✪ Ariel 3½hp

Bat No. 2 ✪ BSA 3½hp ✪ Zenith Gradua ✪ Rudge Multi

Triumph 3½hp ✪ Lea-Francis ✪ Royal Enfield V-twin

Scott 3¾ Two Speed ✪ Clyno ✪ Douglas 2¾hp ✪ Wooler

The Pioneers

No one can really say where the motorcycle began, for it was the result of many simultaneous experiments in different countries.

Most historians date the motor industry from 1885, when two Germans, Daimler and Maybach, put the first really practical four-stroke engine into a wooden test-vehicle that they called the Einspur. As it had two wheels, albeit with a small pair of supporting wheels on each side, this can be said to be the first motorcycle, although Daimler and Maybach themselves saw it simply as a stepping stone to building the first car. But the British industry also got off to a flying start for, at around the same time, British inventor Edward Butler put forward his design for a twin-cylinder tricycle, which, in featuring electric ignition and a proper carburettor, was in many ways more advanced than Daimler's. Sadly, as with so many bright ideas before and since, ambitious plans to go into production failed to materialise, and Butler went no further than a prototype.

What is beyond dispute is that the first commercially successful motorcycle appeared in 1894, and it was the German Hildebrand and Wolfmüller. In France, De Dion was building tricycles in 1895, closely followed by the Werner motocyclette of 1897.

Unlike developments on the Continent, developments in Britain had been hampered by the Locomotive Acts of the 1860s, which restricted speeds to less than a fast walking pace and were responsible for the notorious red flag that had to be carried in advance of any motorised vehicle. When this law was repealed in November 1896 it was the cause of celebrations that are commemorated to this day in the form of the London to Brighton Run.

The repeal helped a fledgling industry to get started, at first mainly through the efforts of established bicycle manufacturers eager to get to grips with the new technology. Most of them bought proprietary engines from the French manufacturers, such as De Dion and Minerva, while others obtained a licence to build the De Dion or Werner machines.

There were many snags in getting the industry off the ground. Even if the basic design was sound – and many were not – public acceptance of the motorcycle was a long time coming. To start with, they were invariably expensive to buy and running costs were high. There were no wayside fuel stations, and the road more often than not consisted of an unmetalled, rutted track covered with mud and horse manure. Speed traps were common, and there

Before the turn of the century, would-be manufacturers had experimented with a host of alternatives. The forecar, an early attempt to accommodate a passenger within a tricycle layout, enjoyed a brief vogue. The model made by Humber was one of the most successful.

were many other legal restrictions on the pioneer motorist.

Unreliable, low-powered engines were the norm, and this helped to delay the development of a proper motorcycle, since what was euphemistically termed 'light pedal assistance' was looked on as essential not only for starting but also for going uphill or even into a headwind. As a result, it was a long time before motorcycles dispensed with pedalling gear completely and became something other than motorised bicycles.

The need to retain the pedalling gear, as well as a natural desire to experiment, led to considerable debate about such matters as the location of the engine. There were many weird and wonderful alternatives, while the problem always on the designer's mind was the dreaded 'side-slip', or skidding, a natural result of poor road surfaces, skinny tyres and what was often a very high centre of gravity.

It is perhaps surprising that the motorcycle evolved at all, but all the trials and tribulations must have been worth it for the occasional opportunity to fly effortlessly and unhindered down an open road.

The pioneer motor trade developed from the bicycle dealers and blacksmiths who served an earlier generation. In 1913 Douglas dealer Frederick Turpin (above) also offered Scott, Clyno, Premier and Bradbury machines from as little as 25 guineas. Almost 100,000 motorcycles were registered that year.

A pioneering spirit helped the early enthusiasts over the inevitable tribulations, while early magazines and books (right) were soon on the market to advise on everything from the choice of a machine to tackling roadside repairs.

The ingenuity and the enthusiasm of the designers knew no bounds, while the astonishing flexibility of the pioneering engines allowed them to triumph, despite the fact that most bikes lacked such items as a clutch or gearbox. Machines were generally started by a run and bump, and stalled when stopping, which initially limited their appeal to fit (and tall) young men.

Even so, the fledgling British industry produced some astonishing designs, including the world's first four-cylinder motorcycle. Development of the Holden began in 1896 and a water-cooled version was launched in 1899. With an engine that ran at just 400rpm and a power output of some 3bhp, it completed a run of over 100 miles in 1900.

Such experiments apart, it was clear for the most part that developments would centre mainly on single-cylinder side-valve engines with simple air cooling.

Clearly displaying its bicycle origins, the layout of the motorcycle settled down in the early years of the 20th century. It became the convention to have the engine in the position of the bottom bracket, with a simple belt drive to a large rear-wheel pulley, as on this 1903 Kerry. Pedals were still necessary to start off, as there was no clutch, and to assist the engine when the going got tough.

It was not until the beginning of the 20th century that machines that were recognisably related to the modern motorbike became generally available on the British market. The French Werner helped to pioneer the conventional position of the engine in place of the bicycle's bottom bracket, and many British manufacturers had their own variations on the theme. Although many of these early machines were too primitive and too demanding to appeal to anyone but committed and well-heeled enthusiasts, the majority went surprisingly well, and were capable of turning in some astonishing speed and endurance records.

The problem of accommodating a passenger, which had led to strange inventions such as the trailer and forecar, was now resolved mainly by the equally mechanically odd sidecar. This, however, had the significant advantage that the passenger was separated from all the fuss and dirt of the motorcycle itself.

While road racing had been a spur to development in mainland Europe, British roads could not legally be closed for motor sport. As a result, many of the early speed races and competitions were undertaken on the banked tracks built as a result of the cycle boom, or on the driveways of private estates. This contributed to the popularity of such events as reliability trials and hill-climbs. But the bar to pure

War and peace: the sidecar (left) developed as family transport, but soon found a new use on the battlefields of Europe (above), where the 'Trusty Triumph' single became the staple military machine.

road racing was removed with the construction of Brooklands in Surrey, a banked road track designed by Holden, where the first full-scale motorcycle race was held in 1908. A year before that, an even more significant event had taken place. With its own legislature, the Isle of Man was not subject to mainland restrictions, and as a result had been the site of the first Tourist Trophy – effectively a cross between a race and a reliability trial – in 1907. Won at little over 36mph, it was a small beginning for a race that would become a dominant force in the British industry, and then the world.

Before World War I, racing and commercial pressures had forced the pace of technological change, and most of the features of modern motorcycles had been tested in some form. Although the majority of machines still used a direct belt drive linking the engine and rear wheel, the advantages of a variable gear had been more than amply demonstrated, while numerous ingenious suspension systems had been tried. Chain drive, shaft drive, telescopic forks, four-valve engines, four-cylinder engines, water-cooled engines, overhead-camshafts and many other features recognisably similar to those of modern machines had all been seen – many of them British inventions. And with the outbreak of war, the light, manouevrable motorcycles produced by the leading British manufacturers found a host of applications, which earned them respect in the most taxing conditions in history.

The following pages tell the story of the many and varied experiments that ultimately led to the development of the modern form of the motorcycle. The story features such well-known names as BSA, Norton and Triumph, which went on to become legends of the industry in their own day – as well as the many that failed to survive those early pioneering days.

Humber Trike

Based on a pioneering French design, the tricycle format of the Humber offered greater stability than a two-wheeler on the rough roads of the day. It was one of the first truly successful motorcycle designs, produced in a variety of capacities both by the original makers and licensees such as Humber.

Humber Trike (1898)

Years in production: 1898

Engine type: single-cylinder side-valve four-stroke

Compression ratio: 4:5

Transmission: direct gear drive to rear axle

Top speed: approx 40mph

In the very early days of the motor industry there was a host of inventors prepared to make all manner of fanciful claims for their designs – and a host of entrepreneurs who were only too eager to prosper from them. Most of these schemes came to nothing, but where a few succeeded, the industry began. One such scheme was the brainchild of Humber.

Humber was established as early as 1868 by one Thomas Humber, whose aim as a bicycle pioneer was to build the best quality machines possible at his works in Beeston, Nottingham. In this aim he succeeded, and although he quit the business in 1892, before it had any connection with powered transport, his bicycles had already achieved a fine reputation. In 1884 they had pioneered the first diamond frame, a design that would become almost universal for bicycles, as well as forming the basis of most pioneer motorcycles.

During the cycle boom of the 1880s, Humber was built into a very large company indeed, with works in Beeston, Coventry and Wolverhampton – partly because of its association with an entrepreneur named Hooley, a man with a somewhat shady reputation for financial dealings. It was typical of the time that such men prospered, and a few years later two more appeared on the scene. These were Edward Joel Pennington, an American given to impossibly extravagant claims on behalf of the motorised gadgets and patents he peddled, and Harry Lawson, an English entrepreneur.

At Lawson's behest, in 1896 Humber started work on a number of prototypes of an experimental machine. Although Humber and Lawson spent a great deal of money, none of the prototypes ever came to anything. The most promising was a version of a Humber tricycle that had a single rear wheel and passenger seat between two steerable front wheels, and a De Dion engine mounted behind the rear wheel. In the years before 1900, the French De Dion company was the biggest name in proprietary engines, which were used by many fledgling manufacturers in Britain. The company was also behind the extremely successful French De Dion and Leon Bollée tricycles.

Harry Lawson's Motor Manufacturing Company (MMC) acquired the sole rights to the De Dion engine, which he built in Coventry. He also held the rights to the three-wheeler, which he passed on to Humber in 1896. This time the experiment was successful, and although the Humber works were destroyed in a fire soon after the first machines were completed, the company was by then firmly established as a motorcycle manufacturer.

In 1902 the firm (by now under new management) acquired the rights to the P&M design and started to make this as the Humber Beeston. They had also begun experiments with their first cars, which would prove even more successful. Humber continued to build motorcycles up until 1930, and in 1911 even won the first Junior TT held over the Mountain Circuit. Some years later, motorcycle production ended as a result of the depression, and the bicycle business was sold to Raleigh. But under the ownership of the Rootes group the Humber name would live on for a century after the company was founded.

The De Dion-based engine design (left) owed a great deal to pioneering Daimler, who made the first truly practical internal combustion engine. The aluminium alloy crankcase, radial finning and long holding-down bolts were De Dion innovations. Drive to the rear axle was by spur gear and pinion.

Matchless

Matchless was one of the true pioneers. Having become one of the first manufacturers in Britain, the firm really established themselves in 1907 by winning the single-cylinder class of the inaugural Isle of Man TT race. The company would go on to become one of the mainstays of the British industry.

Theirs was a familiar tale, moving from bicycle manufacture to motorcycle production, although, unlike most of their rivals, they were not based in the Coventry or Birmingham area, but in Plumstead, London. The firm was founded by H H Collier, whose young sons Harry and Charlie joined him before the end of the 19th century. Their first motorcycle had its French-made engine bolted under the front downtube of a bicycle-type frame. This appeared in 1899.

In 1902-3, their first production machines appeared. The early machines had the engine slung under the front downtube, below the steering head. There was much experimentation with the engine position, including between the seat tube and rear wheel. Stability was improved by a later model, in which the engine moved to the inside of the downtube. This machine used a version of the popular $2\frac{3}{4}$ hp De Dion engine, manufactured under

licence by the Motor Manufacturing Company (MMC). Ignition and carburation were primitive, using a total-loss battery and coil arrangement, and spray carburettor, but the models sold well enough to see further development, with an engine that finally settled in the centre of the frame, ahead of the pedals.

Juggling act (above): early engines had few automatic functions, so a host of tank-top levers was necessary to keep the ignition and carburation on song.

The 1902-3 model (below) has its engine placed under the front downtube, but the Collier family experimented with a number of different layouts in the pioneering years. The bicycle origins of the frame are clearly visible.

The inventive Colliers continued to experiment, and in 1904 launched a tri-car, with a pair of front wheels and single rear wheel. It was designed to provide transport for a passenger who sat ahead of the driver, between the wheels. The tri-car failed to sell well, and was dropped in 1905. But Matchless had already launched a new motorcycle that year, using the new V-twin engine built by fellow Londoner J A Prestwich (JAP) of Tottenham.

Transmission was by the conventional direct belt, but where the model really showed the forward thinking of its makers was in its pioneering front and rear suspension. That at the front was by leading-link forks, while at the rear it consisted of a swinging fork with spring box under the saddle.

On such a model Harry Collier – no mean sporting rider – represented Britain in an international race in France. The following year, both he and his brother Charlie were entered, with Charlie coming third.

Charlie Collier won a famous TT victory on a model powered by a single-cylinder overhead-valve JAP engine, which was exhibited in 1907 together with a new spring-frame V-twin and a racing model. Harry Collier had recorded the fastest lap in the 1907 TT, and together the

The Collier name is cast into the crankcase of the side-valve V-twin. A three-speed hub gear is fitted, although there was a six-speed variant that combined a variable pulley and movable rear wheel, similar to both the Rudge Multi and the Zenith Gradua.

brothers continued their winning ways, taking first place in the 1909 and 1910 TTs, while in 1908 a V-twin topped 70mph at the newly opened Brooklands racetrack.

As World War I approached, Matchless continued to develop their product. In 1912 they introduced a three-speed hub gear, and also began making their own engines. Surprisingly, they produced almost no motorcycles during the war, although the factory made an enormous contribution by manufacturing parts for munitions and aircraft. They would go on to become one of the significant marques of the British industry.

By the time that the 1912 V-twin (below) was built, motorcycle design had settled into a conformity – although on the way, Matchless had pioneered advanced suspension and many other features, including the dropped frame tube to lower the seating position. While the V-twin was a tourer, the company's racing machines had dominated many important events prior to 1910.

Matchless 5hp V-twin (1912)

Years in production: 1912

Engine type: V-twin side-valve four-stroke

Bore and stroke: 85 x 85mm

Compression ratio: 4:1

Capacity: 770cc

Transmission: direct belt drive with three-speed hub gear

Top speed: approx 60mph

Triumph 3hp

With its rebirth in the modern era, Triumph has become the longest-lived of the British marques. This dates from the 1905 3hp, the first machine entirely of Triumph's own manufacture, a true landmark in the history of the British industry.

Like so many other pioneers, Triumph was originally a bicycle company, founded in 1885 by a German expatriate, Siegfried Bettman. Together with a fellow German, engineer Mauritz Schulte, he set up in business in Coventry, choosing a company name that he believed would appeal to French and German buyers as well as the English. In fact, in the year that Triumph built its first motorcycle, a subsidiary German company was set up in Nuremberg, only separating in 1929.

That first Triumph motorcycle was designed in 1902 and used a proprietary Minerva engine in what was essentially a bicycle frame. The next, in 1903, had a JAP engine in a similar frame, but sales were slow and Triumph decided that they needed to build their own power unit. Designed by Schulte in 1905, and backed by considerable commitment on Triumph's part, it was a simple side-valve single, but used a much more advanced design than the engines they had been fitting.

Practical features abounded. At a time when many rivals relied on hit-and-miss 'automatic' inlet valves opened by suction, Triumph's was operated by a cam, a mirror of that used for the exhaust. The strong bottom end included proper main bearings, rather than bushes, and a heavy flywheel to keep the engine running smoothly through the power pulses.

One of the key developments was a proper magneto. While earlier pioneers had relied on the unreliable and potentially dangerous hot-tube ignition, electric ignition was starting to find favour. However, the early systems often relied on a coil and trembler powered by an 'accumulator' or battery to provide a spark. As there was no charging system, the battery had to be recharged after a run. Some of the early Triumphs used this system, but the 3hp offered the option of a magneto for the first time. Starting was improved and the rider was freed from reliance on a well-charged battery.

The 3hp model still used a bicycle-type frame with direct drive to the rear wheel, but soon demonstrated its advantages to would-be customers. With rigid, braced forks, it was light and manouevrable. The next year it gained a stronger frame and a primitive form of front suspension in the form of Triumph's own design of fork. This pivoted fore and aft, controlled by a large horizontal spring.

The engine was also improved, and in the first Isle of Man TT, held in 1907, J Marshall and F Hulbert took second and third place in the single-cylinder class. Sales took off and reached a level of some 20 a week. From such simple beginnings, Triumph was on the way to becoming one of the major forces of the British industry.

The simple side-valve engine (right) would cruise at around 35mph and return a top speed of around 50mph for a miserly 90mpg. This model is equipped with battery ignition.

Triumph 3hp (1905)

Years in production: 1905-07

Engine type: single-cylinder side-valve
  four-stroke

Bore and stroke: 78 x 76mm

Compression ratio: 4:1

Capacity: 363cc

Transmission: direct belt drive

Tyres (front/rear): 2 x 22in/2 x 22in

Wheelbase: 49in

Weight: 125lb

Top speed: approx 50mph

Little more than a heavyweight bicycle (around 125lb) with a 363cc engine fitted ahead of the pedalling gear, the 3hp model was the first true Triumph motorcycle. For its period, it was remarkably advanced and reliable, helping to set the company on the road to fortune.

P&M

P&M was one of those firms that, having had a great idea, stayed with it and refined it so that it effectively became the company's trademark. In the case of P&M this was so much the case that the idea lasted for 66 years.

The great idea dated back to 1900, when Joah Carver Phelon went into business with one Harry Rayner to develop a motorcycle. In those days, there was considerable debate and experiment into how to accommodate a motorcycle engine within the confines of a bicycle-type frame, and many were the weird and wonderful alternatives. Phelon's solution was to remove the front downtube from the frame and fit the engine in its place. It was an attractive solution. Not only was the engine – potentially at least – as strong as the tube it replaced, but it was well out in the cooling air, the centre of gravity was low and the drive was conveniently positioned. More of Phelon's forward-thinking was evident in the choice of chain drive to the rear wheel, when almost all manufacturers opted for belts.

The tank-mounted lever controls the two-speed gear.
Pulling it back engages the clutch connected to the low-ratio sprocket; pushing it forward engages the high-gear chain.

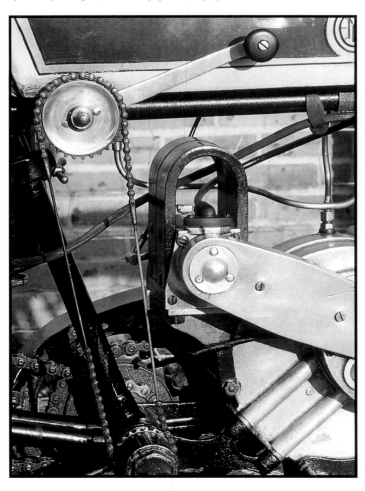

Despite the machine's promise, the Yorkshire-based company was tiny and had limited resources. Their first engines were fitted to frames made by Humber, but from 1902 the design was licensed to Humber themselves. In this form the motorcycles proved very successful, achieving distinction in the 1902 RAC trials, using a 344cc engine with automatic inlet valve.

Phelon's original partner died in 1903, and in 1904 he went into a new partnership called Phelon and Moore, with the trademark P&M of Cleckheaton, Yorkshire. At Moore's instigation, P&M renegotiated the Humber licence, with a view to using the engine/frame design in conjunction with a new two-speed gear.

Again, the new model was well ahead of most of its rivals. The two-speed ratios were achieved by using a pair of primary chains and engine sprockets, together with expanding clutches that enabled the drive to be disengaged. This was a major advance in the days when

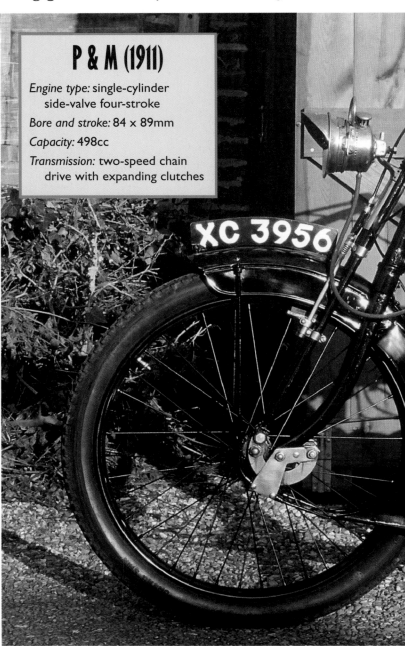

P & M (1911)

Engine type: single-cylinder
side-valve four-stroke

Bore and stroke: 84 x 89mm

Capacity: 498cc

Transmission: two-speed chain
drive with expanding clutches

most machines had to be bump-started after every halt. A patented half-compression device was also fitted to make starting easier – a feature that the model's descendants would retain over half a century later.

Mechanical inlet valves were introduced in 1910, with other refinements, but the two-speed gear remained. P&Ms were very reliable and performed well in trials and endurance tests. This was to stand the firm well in the future.

P&Ms were the Royal Flying Corp's service model of choice in World War I. Both solo and sidecar models were auctioned off in 1919.

Civilian production of a similar machine returned in the 1920s, and there would be some creditable trials and racing performances. From 1926, the trademark 'Panther' was adopted, and although the years wrought many changes, when the last Panther left the Cleckheaton works in the 1960s, it still used its engine in place of the front downtube.

The steeply inclined engine (left) runs from headstock to bottom bracket of the frame, in place of the normal downtube. As well as having strong castings, high tensile steel rods run the length of the engine to provide additional stiffness.

P&M's original design dated to a time when manufacturers were still undecided about where to put the engine. Such was their foresight that it helped to establish both their own firm and Humber, while the addition of a workable two-speed gear in 1904 again put them well ahead of the competition.

Singer

Among the early pioneers, Singer was an innovative company whose products were soundly designed and beautifully engineered. But like several of its contemporaries, Singer was a manufacturer of cars as well as motorcycles, and although its two-wheelers were deservedly popular, they lost out when the company decided to concentrate on the more profitable end of the motor business.

Based in Coventry, like so many of the early manufacturers, Singer first made a name for themselves with a product called the Singer Motor Wheel. This was a novel idea, first developed before the end of the 19th century, at a time when manufacturers were experimenting with all kinds of solutions to the problem of where to put the engine in a conventional pedal cycle frame. The motor wheel was the brainchild of a company called Perks and Birch, who patented it in 1899. It included a complete engine, together with tank and transmission, built inside a wheel that would fit into the rear forks of an ordinary bicycle.

Singer, already makers of bicycles and tricycles, took over the patent and refined the design. Fitted to the rear wheel of a bicycle or the front wheel of a tricycle it became popular at once and sold well. Simple to operate, the 208cc

Pioneer ergonomics dictated placing the controls where it suited ease of manufacture (left.). Levers fitted to the tank were not necessarily easy for the rider to operate, but with little traffic, it was possible to take time to make running adjustments.

engine had a single speed control lever that was fitted to the handlebars, while the ignition used what was probably the first effective motorcycle magneto. The pedalling gear of the bicycle was left in place so that the rider could use it for starting, and for the 'light pedal assistance' that most pioneer motorcyclists were expected to provide on hills.

Singer had always made all the components themselves, and after 1904 it was a short step to making a motorcycle of more conventional appearance. This was similar to well-established contemporary designs, such as the Triumph, and placed a single-cylinder engine centrally in front of the pedalling gear of the bicycle, using direct belt drive to the rear wheel. The magneto moved to the front of the engine, and carried a distinctive external horseshoe magnet. With its flat tank, its pepperpot silencer and strutted, braced girder forks, this was almost the archetypal pioneer layout.

Several variations on the theme appeared, including 350cc two-strokes and, later, water-cooled four-strokes. The most popular were the conventional air-cooled side-valves of 299, 499 and 535cc.

Singers were entered in competition, but with limited success. One of the $2\frac{1}{2}$ hp models came fifth in the Isle of Man TT in 1913, but racing was never their forte. All were popular, usable machines, and the larger models were often fitted with sidecars of the open, wicker construction then popular. Meanwhile the Singer car had developed from early experiments with threewheelers, and by World War I had become the company's mainstay. After several mergers, the Singer name lived on in the British car industry until the 1960s, long after the motorcycles were forgotten. As for the Singer Wheel, an almost identical concept made a brief resurgence in the years after World War II, as part of the cyclemotor boom – with the BSA Winged Wheel as perhaps the best known. A similar engine in the wheel even appeared as a Honda moped of the 1960s.

Light but sturdy, Singer's pioneer machines were beautifully engineered by a company that made all the components in-house.

Singer (1911)

Years in production: 1904-15

Engine type: single-cylinder side-valve four-stroke

Capacity: 299cc

Compression ratio: 5.5:1

Gearbox: direct belt drive

Wheels and tyres: 26 x $2\frac{1}{2}$in

Top speed: approx 45mph

Norton 3½hp

Few individual machines become so famous as to acquire their own nickname. But the Norton 3½ hp, called 'Old Miracle', amply justified its name, with over 100 records and a performance that, with a top speed in excess of 80mph, was hardly to be credited from an unsophisticated, belt-drive single.

The first Nortons were made in 1902, the product of James Lansdowne Norton, bicycle fittings manufacturer of Birmingham. The first machine to bear his name used an imported clip-on engine, and although it was effectively a power-assisted bicycle, Norton was a man of high standards, and the model was neatly constructed. It was not long before improvements and experiments with a variety of other proprietary engines were on the way.

One such machine was powered by a V-twin Peugeot engine; it was aboard a privately entered example of one of these models that H Rem Fowler won the prestigious twin-cylinder class of the first-ever Isle of Man Tourist Trophy in 1907, as well as setting the fastest lap.

It was partly in response to this famous victory that Norton began to build his own engines, starting at the 1907 Stanley Show with his Model No.1, the Big Four. A 633cc side-valve single, it would continue in production (albeit heavily updated) until 1954.

In 1909 Norton introduced a smaller version. Rated at 3½ hp, it was actually of 475cc, with 82 x 90mm bore and stroke. A new model appeared two years later for the 1911 Senior TT races. This had a 490cc engine derived from the relatively long-stroke 79 x 100mm dimensions that would grace Nortons for a further 50 years. Again called the 3½, it would grow into the Model 16 and then the immortal 16H.

In 1911, that first year of the new model's appearance, Norton himself rode one of the new machines in the TT, but as he was in poor health this was far from wise. As in previous years, he failed to place, but others had already begun setting records with the machine. Dan Bradbury was the first rider of a machine under 500cc to top 70 mph, while in 1912 Jack Emerson won the 150 mile Brooklands TT by some 13 minutes, setting a string of records in the process.

Simplicity was part of the keynote of Norton's success. The circular crankcase contained full-circle flywheels and a substantial big-end. The head and barrel were cast in one, but had substantial finning and a good clear passage for cooling air, with a simple sweep of the exhaust pipe providing the most efficient path for the emerging gases. The rest of the machine followed the normal Norton pattern of long, low frame, girder forks and flat tank, which the factory claimed

Simplicity characterises the engine (left), with smooth surfaces and easy curves. Rugged construction, plus the easiest possible passage for the gas and a cooling airflow are the secrets of its performance and reliability.

Simplicity as an art form. The length of the frame emphasises the spareness of the layout, consisting of little more than engine, drive belt and the lightest possible cycle parts.

The tyre inflator atop the flat tank is a reminder of the hazards of pioneer motorcycling, while having to operate the tank-mounted hand-pump for engine oil was an accepted part of the rider's art (right).

'set the fashion in the motorcycle world'. Whatever the truth of this, the handling was legendary. Norton had already started to use the slogan 'The Unapproachable', which would stay with the company down decades of racing success. In 1913 Norton advertised themselves as holding seven world records, including the mile at over 73mph. Such phenomenal performance was little short of a miracle.

When war intervened, production went into temporary abeyance. Although the Norton 3½hp was resurrected in 1919 little changed from before, it was as the Model 16 that the next part of its story would be written.

Norton 3½hp (1911-14)

Engine type: single-cylinder side-valve four-stroke

Bore and stroke: 79 x 100mm

Capacity: 490cc

Tyres (front/rear): 2½in clinchers

Brakes: rim

Top speed: 80+mph

Wilkinson TMC

Wilkinson's luxurious four-cylinder touring motorcycle must surely have been the most sophisticated machine of its age – and certainly the most comfortable, with a specification that included front and rear suspension and a car-type upholstered seat. The product of the old-established and prestigious Wilkinson Sword Company, it demonstrated engineering of the highest quality and a design that was years ahead of its time.

Wilkinson had dabbled with motorcycle manufacture as early as 1903, chiefly as a way of occupying its workforce when military contracts were at a low ebb, but that had been a relatively simple machine using a proprietary single-cylinder engine.

The model that next took their fancy, in 1908, was quite different. Young designer P G Tacchi had patented a design for what he intended as a military scouting machine, equipped with a Maxim machine gun on the handlebars. As military suppliers, Wilkinson were attracted by the scheme, and despite their failure to win an army contract they decided to persevere.

The original Tacchi design had used a proprietary V-twin engine and forks, but in many other respects, including the rear suspension, it resembled the Wilkinson that followed. Called the Touring Auto Cycle (TAC), it was shown in public

during 1909 and was aimed at the civilian touring market. Powered by a 676cc four-cylinder air-cooled engine, it featured a car-type clutch and three-speed gearbox, plus shaft drive. There was a new fork designed by Tacchi, which used quarter-elliptic leaf springs, as at the rear. Steering was either by long, swept-back handlebars, or a car-type steering wheel. The machine was greeted enthusiastically, and production began at Wilkinson's works in West London.

A couple of years later there was a major change to the design, with the launch of the Touring Motor Cycle (TMC).

Luxuriously equipped and with sophisticated design, Wilkinson's four-cylinder machines were dubbed the 'two-wheeled Mercedes' but were only ever built in small quantities. This example has minor modifications to the lubrication and cooling systems, a legacy of its use to pull a sidecar.

The massive Jones speedometer is positioned for maximum visibility.

The most obvious alteration was the use of a water-cooled side-valve engine, now of 848cc. There was also a return to a more conventional type of proprietary front fork, and there were numerous detail changes to the transmission and frame.

In fact, there were many changes throughout the development of the Wilkinson, which was hand built in small numbers. A larger, 996cc engine was offered in 1913, mainly for the benefit of the potential sidecar user. There were also internal changes to the engine and different bodywork.

World War I, and the ensuing rise in demand for armaments, meant that Wilkinson suspended production. But rights to the TMC, and a light car that Wilkinson had also been working on, were taken over by Ogston, another West London firm. When peace returned, Ogston concentrated their efforts on the car, while Wilkinson turned the factory over to making garden tools – a practical example of swords into ploughshares. Only a couple of hundred Wilkinson fours had ever been made, but their demise spelt the end to one of the most interesting pioneers of the British industry.

Wilkinson TMC (1909-16)

Engine type: four-cylinder water-cooled side-valve four-stroke (TMC)

Bore and stroke: 60 x 75mm

Capacity: 848cc

Transmission: car-type three-speed gearbox and shaft drive

Carburettor: Stewart Precision

Suspension: Saxon front forks, quarter-elliptic rear springing

Top speed: approx 50mph

Ariel 3½hp

A chain-driven magneto (right), positioned in front of the engine, and a float carburettor were two features that Ariel offered from the first; they helped to set Ariel ahead of the competition.

In 1870 James Starley and William Hillman patented the first wheel to use tensioned wire spokes. Much lighter than previous built-up wheels, it was used to build a patented penny-farthing bicycle that they called Ariel, after the mythical sprite of the air. Justly popular, the bicycle company grew until, in 1896, Starley merged his company with another engineering concern, Westwood Manufacturing, in order to make bicycle components. The resulting company was also closely associated with Swift, another pioneering motorcycle manufacturer which was based in Coventry.

The first motorised Ariel came two years later, in the form of a quadricycle, or quad, effectively a four-wheeled bicycle using a French De Dion engine driving the rear axle. This was soon modified into a motor tricycle, based on the De Dion design but with a number of improvements – principally that of carrying the engine nearer the centre of the frame to improve roadholding. Carefully designed and well constructed, the tricycles sold in large numbers.

The first Ariel motorcycles appeared in 1902, and were somewhat in advance of most of the competition. Using an engine manufactured by Kerry, they featured proper carburettors and magneto ignition, at a time when unreliable surface carburettors and hit-or-miss hot fuse ignition was the norm.

The company itself was called Components Ltd, and was now run by Charles Sangster, a man with a pioneering spirit. Under his guidance, Ariel was chosen by the Auto Cycle Club (ACC) to represent Britain in the 1905 International Cup Races. Rider J S Campbell won the event at an average speed of over 40 mph. Other early Ariel proving stunts included the 'end-to-end' run from John O'Groats to Lands End, and in 1904 the first Ariel car was launched with a successful ascent of Mount Snowdon.

Even so, sales were slow, despite financial inducements in the form of generous part-exchange offers. This was more a reflection of the high price of a motorcycle in general – then around a year's wages for the average worker – than any failings of the product. Models with 2 and 3½ hp engines were on offer at £25 and £50 respectively.

Ariel 3½hp (1913)

Years in production: 1913

Engine type: single-cylinder side-valve four-stroke

Bore and stroke: 85 x 88mm

Capacity: 499cc

Transmission: direct belt drive

Top speed: approx 55mph

In 1910, Ariel launched a new model with a powerful 4hp side-valve engine built by White and Poppe. This was such a sound design that it would still be in service until 1925. In 1911, Components Ltd bought the design and then undertook to manufacture the machine themselves.

By the beginning of World War I, the range included a 500cc side-valve engine, and a 6hp V-twin. It also embraced the Arielette, a lightweight 350cc two-stroke designed and patented by Sangster himself. Despite advanced ideas such as a kick-start, three-speed gearbox and clutch, the war put paid to this promising design. For a time, more attention was given to cars, under the guidance of Sangster's son Jack. But a number of Ariel motorcycles saw armed service, and by the end of the conflict, the company was well positioned to take advantage of the postwar boom.

Solidly conventional, the Ariel solo was well engineered and set enviable standards of reliability, helping the marque to become one of the industry's leading names.

Bat No. 2

Among the early British pioneers, Bat was perhaps the first to make a serious effort to exploit the publicity available from racing and record-breaking. But their impact was much deeper than this, for the firm also produced some of the most technically sophisticated machines of the era, setting standards that others were soon to follow.

The company was based in Penge, South London. It was founded in 1902 by a Mr Batson, from whose name the bikes took theirs – although it was sometimes said that it was derived from an advertising slogan that claimed they were 'Best After Tests'(BAT). The company's Model No.1 was built using a 2¾hp De Dion engine, and although it was basically a sound product, poor sales resulted in the founder selling the company within two years to one Theodore Tessier, a very able rider. From the first, Bat motorcycles demonstrated their maker's desire to advance the state of motorcycle engineering, for they dispensed with the pedalling gear that most rivals considered an essential backup for when the going got tough, such as riding up hills. They fitted a clutch, well in advance of most of the rest of the industry, and also patented one of the first recorded examples of a fully sprung suspension system. The front fork was a short leading-link design similar in principle to those that would be offered by a number of makers some 50 years later, while at the rear, the saddle and footrests were carried on a subframe. The subframe was suspended on springs from the main frame.

Sales boomed, partly because of the quality of the product, but also because Tessier was a skilled publicist. Launching a single cylinder 3½hp model in the first year after the take-over, he set about racking up a score of over two hundred wins and speed records. V-twin machines using engines supplied by the Tottenham firm JAP followed,

Bat No.2 (1913)

Engine type: V-twin side-valve four-stroke

Bore and stroke: 72 x 78mm

Capacity: 770cc

Compression ratio: 5.5:1

Top speed: approx 75mph

with 650, 770, 964 and 980cc power units fitted. Tessier rode a Bat in the very first Isle of Man TT in 1907, and although it failed to place, the next year's Bat entrant W H Bashall took a second in the twin-cylinder class, also scoring the lap record of 42.25mph. Two years later, in 1910, H H Bowen upped this to 53.15 – but although Bats were regularly entered prior to World War I, this would be the last time that they would figure in the TT record book. Reliability was probably their greatest weakness, for they were technically competent and of proven performance.

The year 1911 saw the introduction of the mountain section at the TT, in response to which many manufacturers

Short leading-link forks were a Bat hallmark from the early days. The principle was similar to that employed by makers such as Greeves half a century later.

fitted gearboxes, including Bat, which offered a two-speed unit as an alternative to the direct belt drive used previously. Both systems continued to be offered in parallel for two years.

By 1913, Bat machines had become more conventional. The spring frame was dispensed with and the new models had a combination of gearbox and belt drive to the rear wheel. World War I then intervened, contriving to dent Bat's fortunes over some machines supplied to Russia's armed services for which they were never paid. This left them in a poor position to exploit the postwar demand for cheap motorcycle transport.

Even so, Bat were in a better position than the fledgling Martinsyde company, which built its first machines in 1919, but foundered in 1923. Bat took over the company and sold Bat-Martinsydes for the next three years. Finally, underfunded and in the face of too much competition, Bat itself succumbed to the inevitable in 1926, after almost a quarter century in which they helped to establish the motorcycle in its modern form.

Bat's 1913 No. 2 Light Roadster was a sports touring machine with a 770cc JAP side-valve V-twin engine.

BSA 3½hp

The company that was to become Britain's largest motorcycle factory was rather late getting started in the new industry. But when they put their first machine on the market, its shrewd combination of the best features pioneered by others helped it to establish a reputation for quality and reliability that formed a solid foundation for BSA's later fortunes.

The company was an old one, for BSA, which stood for Birmingham Small Arms, was originally a gunmaker's trade association with its roots dating back some three hundred years. The BSA company proper was founded in 1861, and made guns for the next 20 years until they took up with the new bicycle industry in 1880. Then the outbreak of the Boer War meant an increased demand for guns, and bicycle manufacture was shelved until peace offered a new market.

During the early years of the century, many of BSA's fellow bicycle manufacturers enthusiastically launched their pioneer motorcycle designs – in fact, BSA made parts for a number of the early motorcycle makers. But although BSA experimented with a proprietary engine fitted into one of their bicycle frames in 1905, it was not until 1909 that they themselves began seriously to develop a product.

The fruits of their labour appeared in 1910, with the launch of their 3½ hp belt-driven single. Part of the reason for waiting may have been to let the market develop. By this time, the early spate of experimentation had settled down somewhat and it must have been clear to BSA that this type of machine was by far the most popular, particularly in the form of the contemporary Triumph – which was already well-established as a practical all-rounder.

The new BSA bore a considerable resemblance to the Triumph, which had been in production for some three years. However, the BSA offered a number of advantages from the outset, and the firm proceeded to improve on them from year to year.

The simple side-valve engine was very close to the Triumph design; indeed, it has been said that several of the components are virtually identical. But in 1913 BSA modified the engine, using a désaxé design in which the cylinder is mounted ahead of the crank axis, the theory being that this results in smoother running and less wear. The carburettor was BSA's own design.

The vintage side-valve displays typical concern for easy valve replacement. Removable caps over the valve heads made it simple to deal with a decoke or a broken valve stem, although the shape of the cast-iron cylinder made it a complex casting.

The racing form of the early BSA dispensed with such touring concessions as the pedalling gear – which was fitted behind the engine – for the ordinary road rider. Its dropped frame tube and lowered saddle anticipated such a move by many of its rivals.

The frame was conventional and clearly based, like its contemporaries, on pedal cycle technology. But in 1912 the top tube was bent down behind the tank to permit a lower seating position – a fashionable and practical change in which BSA anticipated Triumph by a year or so. Where they scored a real mark over their rivals, however, was in the use of a parallelogram-type front fork, with a cantilevered spring – a vastly better suspension system than that offered by most other makers – notably the infamous Triumph fore-and-aft pivoted design.

Other features, such as the hand-pumped total-loss lubrication, were exactly like their contemporaries, although BSA included several practical little refinements designed to ensure fuss-free use. These included a two-speed rear hub gear and conical clutch (altered to a multiplate type in 1913)

at a time when such fitments were unusual, and machines commonly had to be started with a run and a bump, and stalled on stopping.

The model sold well until World War I, and was joined by a larger version aimed at the sidecar market. This became the basis of a military model, and together with a huge demand for munitions helped BSA to grow almost four-fold by 1918 when it was ideally positioned to exploit the postwar boom.

BSA 3½hp (1913)

Years in production: 1910-14

Engine type: single-cylinder side-valve four-stroke

Bore and stroke: 85 x 88mm

Capacity: 499cc

Carburettor: BSA

Tyres (front/rear): $2\frac{1}{4}$ x 26in/ $2\frac{1}{4}$ x 26in

Wheelbase: 55in

Top speed: 50mph

Zenith Gradua

Among the machines favoured by sporting riders in the years before World War I, Zenith machines fitted with the factory's Gradua gear were among the first to offer a really practical variable drive ratio. For a few years they were so successful in hill-climbs and other early events that they were barred from single-gear competitions. The company took this as a compliment and even added the word 'Barred' to their badge.

The earliest pioneer machines relied on direct belt drive to the rear wheel. Although their engines were designed for maximum flexibility, the fixed gear that resulted meant that a machine that could start off and pull up hills easily would have a severely limited top speed. The alternative, adopted by early sporting riders, was to use an adjustable pulley, which could be opened to give a smaller effective diameter,

and hence a higher gear. The only problem that this posed was that the belt tension was lost and it had to be shortened to suit. One early rider's manual devoted two pages to the simple process of climbing a hill, and a similar amount to descending at speed afterwards.

Zenith changed all that with a belt drive system, the ratio of which could be varied on the move. Although technically limited, it was good enough to ensure the marque's success in many important competitions, and having demonstrated the virtue of variable gearing, it paved the way for even more practical alternatives.

Zenith was established in 1904 in Stroud Green, North London. Like most pioneers, they used a variety of proprietary engines, fitted to a bicycle-type frame with direct belt drive. But in 1908, designer Freddie Barnes came up

Zenith manufactured a wide range of machines using the Gradua system. Some versions adopted a chain-cum-belt drive, with a short chain to a separate pulley in front of the engine, as seen on this 1914 V-twin.

LO 3560

The flanges of the front pulley (left) are opened and closed to give a smaller or larger effective diameter.

Belt tension is adjusted by moving the rear wheel back and forth, controlled by the bevel gears (right) at the base of the shaft.

with his development of the variable engine pulley. This had a pair of flanges that could be moved in or out by winding a handle while the machine was on the move. To maintain constant belt tension, the handle was also connected to a linkage that moved the rear wheel forward or backward in a

Zenith Gradua

Years in production: 1908-20
Engine type: single cylinder or V-twin side-valve four-strokes

The 1912 model (below) used a JAP engine single-cylinder side-valve engine made by J A Prestwich in Tottenham, North London.

pair of slots in the rear fork. There were a number of theoretical limitations to this device. Unlike the chain drive that would eventually take over, belts were prone to slip in the wet, while the limited gear ratios still demanded a large and flexible engine to make the best use of them. But with the JAP V-twins fitted to the majority of early Zeniths, the theoretical limitations faded into the background.

Zeniths were originally designed in the shadow of Muswell Hill, one of the steepest slopes in the area, and the Gradua was able to climb it easily and even achieve a hill-start. The system was the key to their success in the popular sport of hill-climbing, run on private slopes with a suitable incline. In 1911, Zenith achieved over 50 major wins, improving on their score the following year. Improvements to the Gradua system followed, including a variation in which a chain transmitted power to a 'gearbox' forward of the engine. Transmission from there on was by Gradua belt drive. More sophisticated alternatives had begun to appear, such as the Rudge Multi, while the chain-driven countershaft gearbox would soon eclipse all the pioneers' belt drives.

Zenith continued in production from a new site in South London, making machines powered by everything from a lightweight Villiers-powered two-stroke single to a 1100cc side-valve V-twin. Postwar, they restarted with a 750cc V-twin, but in 1950 ceased production, mainly because of the lack of suitable proprietary engine makers.

Rudge Multi

Rudge Multi (1913)

Years in production: 1912-23

Engine type: single-cylinder inlet over exhaust four-stroke

Bore and stroke: 85 x 88mm (3.5hp) 85 x132mm (5/6hp)

Capacity: 499cc, 750cc

Carburettor: Senspray

Tyres (front/rear): $2\frac{1}{4}$ x 26in/ $2\frac{1}{4}$ x 26in

Top speed (racing model): 83mph

Produced by one of Britain's foremost makers, the Rudge Multi was not just a single motorcycle but a new concept, which represented an important stage in the development of motorcycle transmission systems, taking over from the equally influential Zenith Gradua. Launched in 1912, after the 1911 TT had shown the value of its multiplicity of drive ratios, it would remain in production for 10 years.

Rudge was already a long-established firm. Founded in the 1860s by Dan Rudge, a Wolverhampton publican and keen racing cyclist, Rudge bicycles had patented numerous technical advances and established a name for quality by the time Rudge died in 1880. The firm was kept going through various mergers, and by the end of the 19th century, after a merger with the Whitworth company in 1894, was producing nearly 400 bicycles a day, under the guidance of Charles Pugh, ex-director of the Whitworth company, and John Pugh, works director.

At about this time, Rudge Whitworth undertook a distribution deal with the Werner company of Paris, pioneer motorcycle manufacturers, but it was 1909 before they undertook development of their own first motorcycle. As perhaps Britain's best bicycle maker (a claim that became the company slogan), they were making some 1500 machines a week, and had the resources to undertake all the development in-house.

The Rudge Multi prototype embodied many sophisticated features, several of which were patented, including a new fork shackle and enclosed fork spring, plus an easily removable rear mudguard for dealing with punctures. The engine was a compromise between a side-valve and an overhead-valve, known as an F-head, but the machine was otherwise conventional, including a direct belt drive to the rear wheel. The first Rudge motorcycle was completed in 1910, in just under two weeks from drawing to metal. Following numerous road tests, including competition, the model went on sale at the end of the year.

In 1911, four Rudges started at the Senior TT, the first year in which the course included the climb over the Mountain. By this time, experiments with proprietary variable gear pulleys made by Mabon had proved the value of such a device on the demanding new course. However, Rudge's first efforts at the TT were not so promising, with two riders retiring, and only a 21st and 22nd place.

Nevertheless, convinced of the value of a variable gear, John Pugh continued development of what was to become the Multi system. Rudge had already patented a clutch that was attached to the engine shaft, outboard of the pulley. To this was added a device that allowed the pulley flanges to open and close. As it did so, the

Patented fork shackles and an enclosed fork spring were Rudge features that would endure for many years.

belt would ride up the pulley, changing the effective diameter of the drive. To maintain belt tension, a linkage went to the rear wheel pulley, or belt rim, which closed and opened to balance the front. This gave ratios between 3.5 and 7.5:1, as well as, in theory, continuously variable selection.

Fitted to the 499cc TT model, the Multi was first entered for the 1912 TT.

The tall, exceptionally long stroke engine gains even greater height as a result of its use of an overhead inlet valve – the 'F-head' arrangement (right). Conventional overhead-valves, as used later, were not popular, as valve breakages were common.

Appearing on a 1913 model of 750cc, the Rudge Multi (below) soon become renowned for its advantage in speed trials and racing, as well as for the average rider.

Although Rudge failed to place, the Multi gear achieved successes at numerous trials and speed events, and was fitted to both the 3.5hp and 5/6hp models. In 1913 a Rudge Multi took second place at the TT, losing only by a narrow margin, and in 1914, Cyril Pullin (who had taken numerous long-standing speed records on his Rudge) won the event. During World War I, Rudge built a few machines for military use, but the main part of the factory was turned over to munitions work. When peace returned, so did motorcycle manufacture, starting with the 499cc Multi in Roadster or TT form. In 1920, the first Rudge to use a three-speed gearbox appeared, but the Multi continued in production until 1923, its cheapness, simplicity and lightness appealing long after the technical superiority of chain drive and a countershaft gearbox had been proved.

Triumph 3½hp

Triumph's pioneering 3½hp (500cc) models probably did more than any other machine to influence the mass acceptance of the motorcycle. Certainly, Triumph were one of the first to undertake mass production on a really major scale, and the reliability of their early models led to their later machines becoming known as 'Trusty' Triumphs.

By 1907, Triumph's solidly engineered 3hp singles had gained the company a good reputation as makers of reliable machines with a fair turn of speed. Part of that reliability came from the Triumphs' integrated design, and in keeping with their principle of controlling all elements of the design, Triumph developed their own twin-barrel carburettor and a magneto system which they fitted for the 1908 season.

It was around this time that the 'Trusty Triumph' nickname first appeared. Although belt drive was still used, Triumph also offered a new transmission system, using a Sturmey-Archer three-speed rear hub, similar to that used on pedal cycles. It was fitted with a clutch, incorporated into the hub.

Light in construction and weight (around 175lb) the 1913 3½hp model was reliable and easy to manage, later earning it the nickname 'Trusty Triumph'.

A simple side-valve design (above), the engine uses direct belt drive to the rear wheel. A hub gear and clutch made for a much easier life than the alternative fixed gear, which meant a run and bump start after every stop.

More models joined the range, including the 225cc two-stroke 'Baby' and sporting variants aimed at the large number of riders who wanted to take part in motorcycle competitions. Triumph's own efforts had paid off with a win for Marshall in the second TT of 1908, and places in 1909 and 1910. Although Triumph machines failed to place in 1911, the marque's endurance had been proved by an epic Land's End to John o'Groats run undertaken by Ivan Hart-Davies, who rode 886 miles in just over 29 hours, the last time such a record run was permitted.

By 1911, the flagship of the range was the 3½hp model. Developed from the earlier 3hp machine, it carried many detail improvements, while the capacity had been increased by some 163cc. More new models followed, until the range embraced a direct belt-drive Roadster, a de-luxe version with a pedal-operated clutch in the rear hub, a sporting TT Roadster and a full TT racing model.

Such machines were capable of high sustained speeds – a TT racing Triumph could top 75mph – while Alfred Catt proved the 3½hp machines' reliability with a phenomenal ride of over 2500 miles in six days, on roads that in the main were little better than cart tracks. His own health was permanently affected, but the Triumph just kept on and on, earning it a place in motorcycle history.

Another development would soon earn the company an even bigger place in history, with a larger 4hp (550cc) version called the Model H appearing just before World War I. The motorcycle mainstay of the war effort, some 30,000 of Triumph's Model H were built, despite the evident weakness of the front fork, the spring of which was prone to snap on rough going, causing collapse of the front end. A favourite despatch rider modification was to strap a heavy leather belt around the fork in case of such a mishap. That failing apart, the side-valve Triumph single lived up to its 'Trusty' nickname, and stayed in use for many postwar years.

Triumph 3½hp (1913)

Years in production: 1906-14

Engine type: single-cylinder side-valve four-stroke

Bore and stroke: 85x 88mm

Capacity: 499cc

Carburettor: Triumph twin-barrel

Tyres (front/rear): 2¼ x 26in/ 2¼ x 26in

Wheelbase: 49in

Top speed: approx 55mph

Lea-Francis

At a time when all motorcycles were something of a luxury item, the products of Lea-Francis were aimed at the top of the market. Concentrating on quality rather than quantity, they built on a solid reputation that had already been established by Lea-Francis bicycles.

Bicycle manufacture had begun in 1895, when Graham Ingoldsby Francis and Richard Lea went into partnership in Coventry. The company's 'safety bicycles' were built to the highest standards, and they had a smart showroom in Piccadilly, London.

Unlike many others, Lea Francis dabbled in car manufacture before undertaking serious experiments with

Lea-Francis (1913-14)

Years in production: 1913-14

Engine type: JAP side-valve V-twin four-stroke

Bore and stroke: 85 x 88mm

Capacity: 430cc

Carburettor: Amac

Transmission: all-chain with two-speed gearbox and multiplate clutch

Top speed: 55mph

Rider conveniences abounded on the quality machines produced by Lea-Francis at their Coventry works. The kickstart, footboards, enclosed chain drive and excellent weather protection were all rarities when the model was introduced, while the patented brakes were supposed to be the best of their kind.

The JAP V-twin (left) was a popular choice of many motorcycle manufacturers, with few weaknesses except for a tendency to overheat. Lea-Francis teamed it with their own two-speed gearbox, which resulted in one of the most likeable packages of the time.

motorcycles, although they did try fitting a proprietary engine to one of the bicycles in 1902. The Lea-Francis car appeared the following year, but it was never a commercial success.

The first motorcycle proper came out in 1912, with a 430cc JAP V-twin side-valve engine. It had a two-speed gearbox and a hefty price that emphasised its quality and concentration on providing the rider with the best of everything. This included excellent weather shielding, with large mudguards, footboards and full enclosure for the all-chain transmission. An under-tray swung forward to act as a stand, and the front brake used a dummy belt rim and friction block. The brakes, like the firm's reflex rear lamp, were patented and said to be 'above suspicion'.

The chain drive and multiplate clutch were both advanced features for the time, when most makers relied on the simple belt. The method of tensioning the chain was also ingenious, for the gearbox was cylindrical, with an eccentric mounting. Simply rotating it in its housing provided a wide range of adjustment – a system that was seen almost 50 years later, when it was taken up for AJS and Matchless lightweights.

All this was the work of designers Norman Lea, the son of the founder, and Charles Ingle, and was very well received by the public despite the price. Norman Lea and Gordon Francis, son of the other partner, entered the new models in several reliability trials in 1913, and won awards in the Six Days' Trial and the Scottish Six Days' Trial, further enhancing the machine's reputation.

In 1914, Lea-Francis exhibited a range of new models with 430, 500 and 750cc JAP or MAG engines. A three-speed gearbox would have gone into production had it not been for the outbreak of war, which interrupted operations. A small number of machines were built for military use, but production virtually came to a halt.

After the armistice, the V-twins returned much as before and continued to win a fine reputation, especially for their performance in the major trials. The three-speed gearbox finally appeared in 1920, but by 1924 the company had decided to concentrate on car production, so motorcycle manufacture was discontinued, leaving a fine reputation behind them.

There was a postscript to the story, however, for young Gordon Francis had joined his father-in-law Arthur Barnett, a former Singer director, in 1919. The motorcycles they built were designed not so much for quality and exclusivity as reliability and economy. Yet the Francis-Barnett marque went on to build its own enviable reputation, including racing and off-road awards, and as part of the AMC Group, survived until as late as 1964.

A famous partnership: the Lea-Francis' tank badge (left) is flanked by the lever for the two-speed gear and the sight glass for the hand-pumped lubrication system.

Royal Enfield V-twin

Right from the beginning, Royal Enfield were proud to associate their motorcycles with their interests in small arms manufacture. 'Made like a gun' became a company slogan, and the pioneer machines gained an enviable reputation for reliability.

Longevity was another of the company's qualities, for having made their first machines in the early years of the century, they were one of the last to founder in the 1970s. The marque attained a kind of life after death, for Enfields are still made in Madras, India, to a design based on an original British pattern.

The first Royal Enfield was a quadricycle made in 1898, and together with tricycles that also used the ubiquitous De Dion engine, these comprised the bulk of the company's output for some years. The Enfield Cycle Company had started as a bicycle manufacturer run by the Townsend family, but in the 1890s was absorbed into the Eadie concern.

Eadie itself was absorbed by BSA in the early 1900s, and Royal Enfield went its own way. Though based in Redditch, Worcestershire, the firm was closely associated with the Royal Small Arms factory in Enfield, Middlesex, for which it made components. It was through this connection that the bike's name and badge, which depicted a rifle with fixed bayonet, originated.

Royal Enfield V-twin (1914)

Years in production: 1913–1920

Engine type: inlet-over-exhaust V-twin
    four-stroke

Capacity: 450cc

Transmission: chain, with cush-drive hub

Top speed: 65mph

The V-twin Enfield became an enduring favourite, whether in solo or sidecar form. With the company's own design of transmission, most were powered by Swiss Motosaccoche engines, the London-built 6hp JAP being an exception.

The first two-wheelers, which appeared in 1901, had a 211cc Minerva engine clamped to a bicycle frame, with twisted-belt drive to the rear wheel. One design had the engine in front of the steering head, another mounted on the front downtube. Both these options soon proved to be inferior to the Werner solution with the engine in the centre of the frame and this was rapidly adopted. An early Enfield idea that persisted through the company's life was the notion of carrying the lubricating oil in a chamber that was cast into the crankcase.

For the next few years, the firm dabbled – rather unsuccessfully – in car manufacture, which meant that it was not until 1910 that real progress on the motorcycle front resulted. This time, the power unit was a 346cc V-twin designed by the Swiss company Motosaccoche. The new machines also included a two-speed gear using paired primary chains like the contemporary P&M or Scott. Another innovation was the use of a rear hub with rubber inserts to provide a cush-drive – again a persisting Enfield feature.

The firm expanded, and started to build its own engines, mostly V-twins of various sizes. Although Enfield regularly entered competitive events such as long-distance trials, it was not until 1914 that they had a really successful venture in the TT, when they fielded a strong team that was placed solidly up the field. Sadly, their best placed rider crashed on the last lap and despite finishing third, suffered a fatal collision at the conclusion of the event.

Soon after this, production was cut short by the war. Their V-twin sidecar outfits were used by the military to great effect as machine-gun platforms, but only in limited numbers. But in the postwar era, the firm's fortunes would rapidly revive, thanks in part to a new departure – a lightweight two-stroke single that had been launched, but not fully exploited before the conflict began.

The Enfield's V-twin engine (above) is an inlet-over-exhaust design, with the advanced feature of automatic lubrication via a double-acting pump. At a time when most makes relied on a hit-or-miss hand pump supplying oil on a total-loss basis, this was a significant advance.

Scott 3¾ Two Speed

One of the true pioneers, Alfred Angas Scott was an original thinker whose contributions to the fledgling motorcycle industry were many and various. Although Scott himself left the company he founded as early as 1919, the two-stroke machines built in the 1920s and 30s were some of the most charming motorcycles of the era, while Scott's ideas continued to influence successors as late as the 1970s Silk.

The list of Scott firsts and patents is extraordinary: including first rotary valves on a two-stroke, first telescopic forks, first kick-starter, one of the earliest parallel twins, and water-cooled motorcycle engines, and one of the first fully triangulated frames.

The man himself was born in 1874 in Bradford. Trained as an engineer, he worked for a time on marine steam engines, the layout of which had an influence on his designs. He began his own experiments early. In 1897, he patented a new type of bicycle brake, and around the end of the 19th century completed a twin-cylinder two-stroke engine, which he used to power the front wheel of his bicycle by friction drive to the tyre.

The experiments continued and the machine gained a transmission to the rear wheel. In 1904, Scott patented the engine design.

The first fully fledged Scott motorcycle was drawn up in 1908, and Scott contracted Jowett brothers, local engineers to manufacture the design for him.

Unconventional in almost every respect, but superbly logical, Scott's water-cooled two-speed twin-cylinder two-strokes won many competitions in the pioneer days and endeared themselves to owners.

Scott 3¾ Two Speed (1914)

Years in production: 1908-26

Engine type: parallel twin-cylinder
water-cooled
two-stroke

Bore and stroke: 73 x 63.5mm

Capacity: 532cc

Carburation: Scott carburettor

Gearbox: two-speed drive by chains
with alternative ratios

Wheelbase: 55½ in

Weight: 250lb

Only a few were made before Jowett decided to concentrate on developing their own car design, but the 333cc air-cooled twin showed most of the features that would become Scott hallmarks. The frame was entirely made of straight tubes, and there was a revolutionary two-speed gear, effectively two entirely separate transmissions giving high or low ratios.

These early machines proved unreliable, but Scott took one to the local motorcycle club's hill-climb in July 1908, carrying off the top award. Three weeks later, at an important annual national hill-climb, he won three top awards, in the Open, Twin Cylinder and Variable Gear classes. The immediate result was that the governing ACU handicapped the Scott on the grounds that its extra firing intervals gave it more power.

In 1910 the machine was the first two-stroke to finish a TT, while the following year it set the record lap. In 1912 it led from start to finish. A further win followed in 1913.

Scott's civilian production continued until 1916, although the founder himself had been actively pursuing military contracts since 1912. His ideas found concrete expression with the design of a military three-wheeled gun carrier, and in 1919 he left the company to concentrate on the design of an unconventional three-wheeler called the Sociable, based on the gun-car. This never caught on and in 1923 Scott contracted pneumonia from which he died. He was only 48, and the company that he founded had many successful years to come.

Clyno

Solid and well-engineered, the Clyno V-twin had reached its peak of development on the eve of World War I. Its qualities were not lost on the military authorities, who adopted the machine as the main standard issue for the Motor Machine Gun Service. Equipped with a sidecar platform and a heavy machine gun, and operating in threes, the machines provided a highly mobile attack force.

Clyno itself had begun manufacturing motorcycles only a few years earlier, but had been formed in 1908 as an accessory maker, based in Thrapston, Northamptonshire. Founded by two cousins called Smith, the outfit's first product was a patented, adjustable inclined driving pulley, from which the firm took its name – a play on the word 'inclined'. The pulley was joined by a range of other useful accessories, and Clyno was soon profitable enough to go into motorcycle manufacture using proprietary V-twin and single-cylinder engines made by the Wolverhampton firm of Stevens, and fittings from Chater Lea in London.

The new machines first appeared at the end of 1909 and were very successful, but a year later there was a problem with the supply of engines. Stevens was another family firm, founded by four brothers, and had been

The massively engineered kickstart quadrant (left) is typical of the Clyno's practical and robust construction.

making engines for the trade since the end of the 19th century. But in 1910 they decided to go into motorcycle manufacture on their own account, as AJS, taking the name from the initials of the senior brother.

As a result, AJS decided to give up manufacturing their V-twin engine, and planned a move to new premises. Clyno simply took over the old Stevens works and machinery. Their machines began to appear from the Wolverhampton works at the end of 1910, the engines at first carrying the Stevens name. The single-cylinder bike was dropped. The next year, a six-model range was on offer, all with the advanced feature of all-chain drive, a kickstart and even a two- or four-speed gearbox offering a choice of alternative chain ratios.

By 1913 the Clyno had become a byword for convenience, with such features as quickly detachable wheels and cast-alloy footboards. With a neat and workmanlike finish, it was robustly engineered, as befitted its favoured role as sidecar haulier. These qualities helped it to win favour at the military trials organised in 1914, and the substantial demand that followed led to the company engaging extra staff and working long shifts to build the armoured combinations. The Clynos were ridden to the south of England and then shipped to France, while from 1917, the Russian army was also supplied with a similar model.

Clyno might have been expected to profit from the postwar boom, but just as they were on the point of launching a new model, their chief designer left for rivals Raleigh. Meanwhile the founder had turned his attention to the light car market. Ultimately this policy spelt doom for the company, as it was unable to ride out the Depression.

Clyno (1914)

Engine type: Stevens/Clyno side-valve V-twin four-stroke

Capacity: 744cc

Carburettor: Amac

Transmission: all-chain with three-speed countershaft gearbox and clutch

Lubrication: semi-automatic, with hand-operated Best & Lloyd pump

Top speed: 55mph

Handsome and sturdy, the Clyno typified the final development of the pre-World War I motorcycle as a practical, comfortable solo or sidecar mount. It was these qualities that won it an important military contract, which saw it built in substantial numbers throughout the war years.

Douglas 2¾hp

Douglas flat-twin motorcycles won undying fame, and fortune, with their performance in World War I, when the company equipped army despatch riders with some 25,000 machines. Technically advanced, they demonstrated the smoothness of an engine type that was adopted by numerous other manufacturers, and used by Douglas themselves as late as 1957.

The Douglas Engineering Company was founded in Bristol in 1882, by Scottish brothers William and Edward Douglas, as a general engineering company and foundry. But the Douglas motorcycle really grew out of the efforts of one Joseph Barter, who founded a company called Light Motors Ltd in nearby Kingswood. Barter had developed a design called the Fairy – which used a horizontally opposed engine of advanced design – after being impressed by the smoothness of this type of engine. Despite its technical advantages, Barter failed to make enough money to enable the firm to

Gear selection is controlled by the handle on top of the tank (left), which selects low or high ratio. Also visible is the hand pump used to supply oil to the engine.

Slim, low and light, thanks to the flat-twin cylinder layout, Douglas models had proved themselves in competition and were well-suited to the demands of wartime despatching.

survive, and in 1907, Douglas took over manufacture of a model based on the Fairy, using direct belt drive. Barter became an employee of the company and helped to develop the machines. His original design had been of 200cc, but under Douglas ownership it was enlarged to 2¾ hp (340cc).

After a couple of years of very limited sales, a turning point came in 1910, with the introduction of a two-speed gearbox fitted under the gearbox and operated by a handle on top of the tank. Belt drive was used and no clutch was fitted – the machine was started simply by pushing off.

The new model soon won an important reliability trial, and before the end of the year scored an important success by setting a record for the Lands End to John O'Groats run. The various technical advances of the Douglas had paid off handsomely, and in 1911 there were more competition successes. In 1912, the engine gained new, mechanically operated valves that gave a power output of some 8bhp. At that year's Isle of Man TT, there were several Douglas entries, which gained an outstanding success, with 1st, 2nd and 4th places, despite the bad weather. Many other racing successes followed and Douglas' fortunes seemed assured.

By the end of 1914, Douglas had sold around 12,000 machines and were well-established, soon becoming one of the most important makers of military machines.

For a small side-valve, the Douglas twin was quick, and being light, it was easy to manhandle. The front plug could short out in the wet, but on the whole the machine was very reliable and smooth running. After the war, a civilian version of the Douglas twin went back into production in 1919, but many ex-WD examples were reconditioned and sold off to the public, giving long and honourable service in peace just as they had done in war-time.

Douglas 2¾hp (1919)

Years in production: 1912-22

Engine type: horizontally opposed (fore and aft) side-valve four-stroke twin

Bore and stroke: 60.8 x 60mm

Capacity: 348cc

Power: 8bhp

Carburettor: Douglas two-lever

Tyres (front/rear): 2¼ x 26in/2¼ x 26in

Weight: 170lb

Top speed: 40mph

Wooler

Despite its date of manufacture, Wooler's unorthodox twin is a true pioneer in spirit. A tiny manufacturer, led by a visionary who seemed to delight in the unusual, the company survived until the 1950s, albeit with a gap of 17 years when no machines were produced. Unusual engine configurations and suspension designs were a Wooler hallmark, as was styling designed to turn heads.

John Wooler built his first motorcycle in 1911, and it set the pattern for the future. The engine was a horizontal single-cylinder two-stroke with a double-ended piston, eliminating the need for normal crankcase compression. The power was transmitted by a long pin that stuck through slots in the crankcase walls external connecting rods to the flywheel. There was a front and rear suspension, way ahead of its time, using a patented plunger system. The patent also covered a fuel tank that enclosed the steering head, supposedly as a means of achieving greater fuel capacity. Using belt drive, there was a pedal-operated device for adjusting the pulley to change gear.

That first machine had a 230cc engine, but by the time it went into production – at the nearby Wilkinson works, as

Wooler had no production facilities – the engine had been enlarged to 344cc. There were numerous minor improvements, including some thoughtful ideas such as knock-through wheel spindles and nuts of only two sizes. That led to a trademark of a double-ended spanner (the only tool needed!) and the word 'Accessibility'. The Wilkinson Wooler was in production until 1913, and manufacture ceased during World War I.

The Wooler that appeared in 1919 was similar in layout but very different in almost every detail of the engine. This was now a

Wooler (1920)

Years in production: 1919-23

Engine type: horizontally opposed (fore-and-aft) inlet-over-exhaust four-stroke

Engine type: single-cylinder side-valve four-stroke

Bore and stroke: 60 x 60mm

Capacity: 348cc

Transmission: initially by variable ratio belt, later by chain drive

Weight: 162lb

Top speed: approx 55mph

350cc four-stroke flat-twin, similar to the popular Douglas, but of inlet-over-exhaust layout rather than a side-valve. The forward-projecting tank was completely redesigned, but the suspension and variable belt-drive systems were there as before.

A real lightweight, the Wooler was also astoundingly economical. During a special test, it achieved an amazing 311 miles on a measured gallon. Entered in the 1921 Junior TT, its performance was unspectacular, coming only 34th, but at Brooklands it broke 29 world records for long-distance endurance. Its 'Flying Banana' nickname is supposed to have been gained after the TT.

After 1923, Wooler fitted new semi-overhead-cam 350 and 500cc versions of the engine; the fuel tank was of conventional shape. For 1926, John Wooler tried a much more conventional machine with rigid frame and fairly conventional girder forks. It had an intriguing overhead-cam 511cc single-cylinder engine, but it was set aside when he bought the ailing Packmann & Poppe company. Moving to Wembley, Wooler's small factory produced a small range of motorcycles until 1930, when it closed down.

As early as 1936, Wooler began work on another incredibly unconventional design, a 500cc transverse four with pistons interconnected by rocking beams to a single big end. News of this broke during the war, but it was not until 1948 that it was seen in the metal. Sadly, this incredibly lightweight design did not proceed beyond the experimental stage.

The horizontally-opposed engine (below) was extremely efficient, covering 311 miles on a gallon of fuel in a special test.

The Wooler gained the nickname 'Flying Banana' from the size, shape and colour of its tank. Despite its unconventional appearance it embodied original thinking that was good enough to gain 29 world records for speed and endurance.

Manufacturers' badges from 1900–1919

Vintage Days

1920-1940

ABC ✪ Levis Popular ✪ Norton 16H ✪ Velocette Two-stroke

Triumph Ricardo ✪ BSA Round Tank ✪ James V-twin

Brough Superior SS100 ✪ Ner-a-car ✪ Cotton TT

Sunbeam Model 90 ✪ Velocette KTT ✪ Norton CS1

Scott Squirrel ✪ Matchless Silver Hawk ✪ Excelsior Manxman

Norton International ✪ Vincent Rapide

Triumph Speed Twin 5T ✪ BSA Gold Star ✪ Rudge Ulster

Vintage Days

Although World War I ended in November 1918, rationing remained in force for some time and it was not until the following year that motorcycle factories were allowed to go back into production.

However, the end of the war coincided with an enormous demand for transport, fuelled by the returning servicemen and women, many of whom had their first experience of motorcycles or cars while at arms.

At first this demand was met by secondhand prewar models or reconditioned military machines, of which there were many thousands – mostly the ubiquitous despatch riders' Triumph single or Douglas twin. Prices were high, there were long waiting lists and fuel was in short supply, but demand was steady. The situation was tailor-made for ingenious dealers and accessory manufacturers, several of whom offered ways to make an old model appear like a new one, or economise with gadgets such as fuel-savers, 'hot' exhausts and plug protectors.

When restrictions on manufacture were lifted, there still remained the problem of limited raw materials, including most metals and rubber. Manufacturing capacity was no problem at all; there was a host of factories that had been forced to turn their attention from profitable and intensive war work to the civilian market. For firms such as Triumph, it was simply a matter of reopening the production lines, but there were many others with no prewar experience, for whom the sellers market was impossible to resist. Factories that had until recently been building aircraft, tanks or even components for the munitions industry began to turn their attention to motorcycles.

Typical of a host of small factories in the immediate postwar years, Sheffield-Henderson was a sidecar maker that assembled machines around proprietary engines from Blackburne – in this case a sporting overhead-valve model.

By the end of 1919 there were 50 new manufacturers and within a couple of years this had risen to over a hundred. More than two hundred models were exhibited at the first postwar Olympia show in 1919. Some of these were gimcrack designs, hastily rushed into production, others were simply 'assembly jobs' relying on bought-in engines, frame parts and running gear. But among the dross there were still gems to be found.

For the most part there was little immediate technical advancement, for the war had demonstrated in the clearest fashion what was worthwhile and what was not. The emphasis tended to be on reliability and convention. BSA, Matchless, Sunbeam and Clyno all showed machines that

Large factories such as railway and shipbuilding conglomerate Beardmore also got in on the act under the name Beardmore-Precision. This is a 1921 350cc model.

Working bikes (right): after the wartime despatch riding experience, motoring organisations were quick to catch on to the practicality of the motorcycle. In 1922, these four RAC patrolmen were equipped with Ivy 250cc two-strokes.

Motorcycles were a staple form of transport in the inter-war years. Lightweights, mostly two-strokes, were favoured by the taxation laws. This 225cc Royal Enfield (below) from the early 1920s was designed to be as cheap as possible but with modernisation lasted right through the Depression, virtually until World War II. It actually became cheaper and cheaper with the passing years.

would have seemed familiar six years earlier. Others were prepared to experiment, such as Royal Enfield with their prototype four-cylinder machine, which failed to go into production. But the star of the show was the revolutionary ABC, manufactured by the Sopwith Aviation company. Representing an enormous technological leap, this above all seemed to presage a new direction for the industry, although the detail flaws and financial muddle that attended its launch were indicative of the age in a less attractive way. Other industrial giants were not far behind, such as the Beardmore combine with the Precision design that again proved to promise more than it delivered.

Production got into full swing in 1920, but the euphoric promises of a year before all too often proved impossible to keep. Many prices were much higher than had been suggested and this would prove the downfall of many a hopeful. A distraction was offered by a brief craze for the scooter, inspired by an American device called the Autoped, which was more of a motorised skateboard than a true scooter. After a couple of years of ingenious but frequently hopeless variations on the theme, the bubble finally burst.

On a more serious note, competitions had also returned in 1919 and were enthusiastically greeted. Hillclimbs, sprints and trials regained all their prewar popularity and

more, while the Isle of Man TT and Brooklands were back in 1920. An ABC won at the first Brooklands event, while Sunbeam, AJS and Levis took the TTs.

The 1920s ushered in what many have called a 'Golden Age' of motorcycling. According to the strict definition, a 'Vintage' bike is deemed to be one constructed before 1930, although since the term was coined just after World War II, perceptions have changed.

As prosperity returned, customers increased in numbers and the successful factories boomed. A host of proprietary engine and component factories including JAP, in London, Villiers, Blackburne and Chater-Lea supported the smaller manufacturers, while the larger ones started a period of expansion and consolidation. Dealers grew larger and more affluent, while motorcycling was seen as socially acceptable for all classes.

On the one hand, a motorcycle could provide family transport or a workaday tool, especially if fitted with a sidecar. Sidecars were built with enough seats for a large family, or purpose-designed for butchers, bakers and even motorcycle dealers to transport their wares. On the other hand, a solo motorcycle was a fashionable accessory for a sporting young man or woman who could afford the very latest 'race replica'.

The basic motorcycle was still recognisably similar to its prewar counterpart – usually a 500cc single cylinder side-valve – turned out in hundreds of thousands by firms such as Triumph and Norton. There were technical improvements in items such as valves, which could now be relied on not to break frequently, and the emphasis was on practicality. There was also a boom in lightweights, partly as a result of taxation, which, after 1921, included a classification on weight – under 200lb and the tax was halved. Simple, lightly built and usually two-stroke powered, such models as the Levis and Royal Enfield offerings were cheap and simple enough to appeal to a new breed of riders.

At the other end of the scale, speeds began to rise and sports machines grew in popularity. In 1924 a Blackburne-engined Chater-Lea became the first 350 to exceed 100mph

Family transport (above): throughout the 1920s motorcycles and sidecar outfits were an eminently respectable means of travelling, and sales boomed.

The Isle of Man TT exercised an enormous influence over manufacturers and public in the interwar years. In a famous incident in 1924 (above) the great Stanley Woods corners his Cotton ahead of Norton's Joe Craig, fallen at Governor's Bridge. Both men would go on to great things, Woods as the most successful rider of his generation, Craig as head of Norton's race shop during their glory days.

Pressed-steel and a Villiers engine were Francis-Barnett's solution to providing low-budget transport. The 1937 Cruiser model offered comfort and cleanliness and was a popular 30s alternative.

at Brooklands, and machines of this size were seen as a real sporting alternative to the 500s. There also grew up a small but significant demand for luxury, high-performance machines, which was satisfied by specialist manufacturers such as Brough Superior and HRD.

Much of the interest in motorcycling was fuelled by the glamour of racing, and in particular the TT, which attracted huge audiences throughout the period. Stars such as Stanley Woods, Jimmy Simpson and Wal Handley were household names, while riders such as Bert Le Vack and Freddie Dixon became famous for their record-breaking exploits, hoisting the world record to almost 130 mph by the end of the decade. Norton and Velocette, among other manufacturers, built their reputations with a string of wins that proved Britain really did build the best bikes in the world. Such new sports as dirt-track (speedway) sprang up, and proved hugely popular with the crowds.

It was only at the end of the 1920s that light cars such as the Morris Minor and Austin Seven began to offer a serious challenge to the motorcycle. There were around three-quarters of a million bikes – a third of the world's total – on Britain's roads in 1929, the year of the collapse of the New York stock exchange.

The shock waves of the Depression that followed soon reached Britain. That year's show had seen the buoyant launch of new luxury models, but economy would soon become the byword. Weaker manufacturers went to the wall, while others turned to more profitable enterprises. Even so, many prospered, partly as a result of cost-cutting and new commercial ideas such as hire purchase. Prices went down and down, reaching rock bottom in 1932, when the annual show at Olympia was cancelled, and a year later the taxation classes were revised to favour small capacity machines. By 1936 the situation had resulted in machines such as the 250cc pushrod-engined Red Panther, offering well over 110 mpg and costing less than £30 cash, payable in weekly instalments of some 33p. Even so, the big Brough Superiors continued to find small numbers of customers at prices of some £180.

Motorcycle sport continued to prosper, perhaps as an antidote to the drab austerity of the times. But commercially things failed to improve. Many famous factories were forced to close or merge – Ariel, the second largest concern in the land, AJS, Douglas and Sunbeam among them. From the mergers that arose at this time, the final shape of the British industry began to emerge.

One of the most significant factors in the shape of the postwar industry was also taking place in the Midlands, where Edward Turner, late of Ariel, now of Triumph, was laying down the form of the Speed Twin, a model that for better or worse would dictate the form of the motorcycle for three decades and more.

But another cloud was gathering, and its influence could be seen in an increasingly significant continental challenge to British sporting supremacy. The great Stanley Woods had switched his allegiance to Moto Guzzi and in 1935 won two

BSA, for a time the biggest manufacturer in the world, got big by making good honest workhorses like the 1934 'Sloper'. The sloping engine and twin fishtail exhausts were fashionable items, but the bike itself was stolid rather than speedy.

TTs for the Italian factory. An even greater challenge was being mounted closer to home. With massive state encouragement, BMW, NSU and DKW were fielding technically advanced racers and record-breakers with the objective of demonstrating Germany's engineering supremacy. With BMWs first and second in the 1939 Senior TT and DKWs placed in both the Junior and the Lightweight, they did just that.

The British answers, including the ambitious supercharged offerings from AJS and Velocette were virtually stillborn, for by the closing years of the 1930s, most of British industry was already gearing up for a conflict that seemed inevitable. Within months Europe was at war, drawing another chapter in motorcycle history to an end.

Norton and Velocette were a British racing double-act throughout the 1920s and 30s. Norton star P (Tim) Hunt pushes off in the 1932 Junior.

ABC

In 1919, many manufacturers who had been involved in war work found themselves facing the prospect of cutting back their activities unless they could diversify into other types of production. One such was Sopwith of Kingston-on-Thames, Surrey, an aircraft company that faced a sudden downturn in demand. Proprietor Tommy Sopwith believed that motorcycle production could be the answer, and turned to the prolific designer Granville Bradshaw for help.

The solution that Bradshaw offered was the astonishingly bold ABC flat-twin – even more extraordinary because the design was completed in a mere 11 days. He had bet the incredulous Sopwith that a prototype could be produced in three weeks – and backed this claim with a deal whereby he staked £100 per day over that time, while Sopwith would pay a similar sum for every day less. As a result, Bradshaw netted £1000 on the deal, an enormous sum at a time when a basic motorcycle could be bought for as little as £50.

An Achilles heel was the valve gear (left), which in its original form proved too weak. Accessory manufacturers offered solutions, but the firm's financial difficulties meant that they were never able to develop the ABC as needed.

A machine built in such a short time might have been expected to be crude, or at the least a copy of an existing design, but the ABC was neither. Its horizontally-opposed twin-cylinder engine employed overhead-valves when most makers, including the slightly later BMW that used a similar layout, stuck with the conservative side-valve layout. It had an integral four-speed gearbox, when many machines still used direct belt drive or, at best, two speeds. Only the chain drive from the gearbox to the rear wheel was perhaps not as advanced as the shaft adopted by BMW.

Part of the reason for this may have been that Bradshaw had decided on a fully sprung frame, which made it harder to accommodate a shaft. The main frame was a double-cradle, ingeniously splayed wide enough to support legshields and footboards, while providing protection for the engine in the event of the bike being dropped. The front fork was a girder design, with quarter-elliptic springing.

At the rear, Bradshaw had designed an early swinging-arm suspension, again leaf-sprung. There were many other features aimed at providing

Rider comfort was a key part of the ABC concept. Front and rear springing, wide footboards and legshields offered a relaxed ride, while sophisticated controls made the ABC easier to ride than most of its contemporaries. Unfortunately, this promising newcomer was beset by teething problems and financial setbacks.

ABC (1919)

Years in production: 1919-25
Engine type: horizontally-opposed twin-cylinder overhead-valve four-stroke
Bore and stroke: 68.6 x 54mm
Capacity: 398cc
Carburettor: Claudel-Hobson
Gearbox: four-speed with H-gate
Top speed: 70mph

Rider convenience: the four-speed gearbox (below) was a real innovation, and the carburettor was simpler to control than that of most contemporaries. Less satisfactory was the lubrication, which had to be changed from wet-sump to a hand-pumped design.

rider convenience and luxury, and when it was launched, the ABC captured the imagination of the reviewers. Light in weight and quiet, the machine had a brisk performance, as well as being comfortable and stable. Orders began to flood in and the French company Gnôme et Rhône were signed up to produce the design under licence.

Then the troubles began. Initially priced at £70, the ABC proved too expensive to manufacture, and the design had to be modified to sort out some mechanical problems. Sales should have begun early in 1919, but when the first machines appeared in May 1920, the price had risen to an astronomical £160, and even at this price the makers were hardly covering their costs.

Only some 2000 were made. Although the ABCs proved capable of winning two speed records in the year they were launched, it soon transpired that the valve gear was weak and prone to breakage. While accessory makers offered cures for its mechanical problems, the factory itself quietly let the unprofitable ABC fade away. The last one made by Sopwith was built in 1923, although Gnôme et Rhône made a few up until 1925. After that it was left to others – especially the flat-twin BMWs – to demonstrate what the concept might have offered.

Levis Popular

As simple as it was possible to be, and cheap with it, Levis' lightweight was typical of the machines that provided everyday transport for the masses in the years just after World War I. But with its quality of engineering, it was also perhaps the best of its kind, and the name Levis went on to become a byword for two-stroke machines that were reliable, light and quick.

Levis motorcycles were made by Butterfields Ltd, an engineering firm started in Birmingham in 1906 by two brothers, William and Arthur Butterfield. Some years later, the firm began experimenting with motorcycle design, and in 1910 successfully tested their own two-stroke engine. The first machine they produced using this engine was only a little more substantial than a bicycle, and very light. With its 196cc two-stroke engine and direct belt drive to the rear wheel, it was capable of some 35mph. For their slogan, Butterfields adopted the Latin phrase 'levis et celer', meaning 'light and fast', and took the name Levis for the name of the motorcycles.

When the machine went into production as the Levis Model 1, the engine size had been increased to 269cc, while there was also a smaller version of 211cc, the Baby Levis. In the years before World War I, Butterfields went on to offer a number of versions of these models, together with a 349cc De-Luxe. In 1914, the 211cc Popular, which had a higher specification than the Baby, was introduced, along with a 175cc Levisette. Under the guidance of works manager Howard Newey, the firm also took its first steps in racing, although there were few events for lightweights.

The war, of course, put paid to much further development, although the firm experimented with engines for the aircraft industry. But in the years immediately after peace returned, there was an urgent need for cheap transport, which Levis stepped in to fill.

Levis had also begun racing again, and in 1920 entered 250cc machines in the Junior (350cc) TT, which included a newly introduced trophy for machines of 250cc or less. But for a crash, Levis was in contention to beat the best 350s; as it was, they still took first, second, and third in the 250cc class, as well as scoring a fastest lap that was 3mph better than the overall speed of the race-winning 350cc AJS.

Simple and light, the 211cc Levis (above) has few frills or unnecessary fittings. An unusual feature is the front downtube of the frame, which splits to allow the exhaust pipe to run centrally.

Unusually for a simple two-stroke of the time, the carburettor (left) supplies only a petrol/air mixture. Oil is provided from a separate reservoir, which feeds directly to the bottom end of the engine.

Levis Popular (1921)

Years in production: 1914-24

Engine type: single-cylinder two-stroke
  with drip feed lubrication

Bore and stroke: 62 x 70mm

Capacity: 211cc

Carburettor: Amac

Tyres (front/rear): 2¼ x 24in/2¼ x 24in

Weight: 118lb

Fuel consumption: 150mpg

Top speed: 35mph

Two years later, Levis won the first Lightweight TT run as a separate event. They also won continental Grands Prix in 1922 and '23.

Among the machines that provided Levis' bread and butter, the Popular was perhaps the most important. It was very simply constructed, with a light frame and forks and a transmission consisting simply of a belt looped around the engine pulley, driving the back wheel. With no kickstart or gears, starting was by pushing or scooting off, using a decompression lever to help the engine turn over easily. A large external flywheel kept the engine running evenly, although it might slow to a fast walking pace when pulling uphill. Brakes were simple, too, with a bicycle-type stirrup brake on the front rim and a heel-operated rear brake working on the belt rim.

But such simplicity did not mean crudeness. The Levis was well-engineered and simple to repair. It even included such sophistication as separate oiling, at a time when most two-strokes relied on a pre-mixed petroil. It was a formula that kept it in production until 1924 – a run of over a decade – when more apparently sophisticated models from both Levis and their rivals had come and gone.

Norton 16H

Tracing its lineage back to 1911, the Norton 16H was by turns a TT racer, wartime despatch machine and family sidecar slogger, in a remarkable career that spanned 33 years. In all that time, the engine's basic layout and dimensions remained unchanged – it was simply that the world moved on around it.

In 1911, the Isle of Man TT included a 500cc Senior class for the first time, and Norton had a new design ready to contest it. A side-valve of 490cc with dimensions of 79 x 100mm bore and stroke, it was listed as the '3½'. Founder James Norton rode one of the firm's entries himself, but failed to place. Yet, the very next year, a similar machine won the Brooklands TT, and three world records in the one event. In 1913, versions on sale included the Brooklands Special (BS) and Brooklands Road Special (BRS), which with their single-speed belt-driven transmission were guaranteed to have lapped Brooklands at more than 70mph (65 for the BRS), while many were in fact capable of exceeding 80mph.

Norton 16H (1922)

Years in production: 1921-54

Engine type: single-cylinder side-valve four-stroke

Bore and stroke: 79 x 100mm

Capacity: 490cc

Compression ratio: 4.9:1

Power: 12bhp

Tyres (front/rear): 3¼ x 26in

Top speed: 78mph

Sporting sidecar (right): the 16H was often linked to a sidecar throughout its long production life, although by the end it was providing family transport rather than race entries.

Lean and low-slung, the 1922 Norton 16H helped to establish a style for fast sporting 'flat-tankers'.

A chain-driven version was developed, but with World War I intervening it was 1919 before the 490cc Norton was back in civilian production. The catalogued Model 16 now featured chain-drive with a three-speed Sturmey-Archer gearbox, and was directly related to the competition machines that were holders of some 21 world records.

In 1920, the year of the first postwar TT, Norton moved to Bracebridge Street in Birmingham. At the TT, Norton's Douggie Brown was pipped to the post by Sunbeam's Tommy de la Hay, but could take satisfaction from knowing that more than half the finishers were riding Nortons.

The next year, Norton launched a new model, called the Colonial. Aimed at the expanding market in less developed areas of the Empire, it had a higher ground clearance than the standard machine, which gained an even lower riding position and a new designation – the 16H ('H'for Home) model. In the TT, although Norton failed to score better than sixth place, it was still the most popular marque represented.

In 1922 Norton's race development effort switched to the newly designed overhead-valve Model 18, but only one works machine was used in the TT, with another privately entered. A further dozen side-valvers were entered. By the next year the side-valver was no longer a works TT mount, but was still a popular private entry.

Out of the spotlight, the 16H found a new role as a popular sporting tourer, with styling and detail changes, such as a switch to a saddle tank, coming slowly over the next decade. The engine was reworked in 1931, but the next major development came in 1936, when after earlier successful trials the army began to place regular orders for 16Hs (modified for off-road work). These orders continued right through the war, with more than 80,000 delivered, spanning a decade in all, and some machines staying in service until the late 1950s.

Velocette Two-stroke

Slim, low and light with a sophisticated engine, the Velocette two-stroke won many admirers, and gave its name to 60 years of successors.

The British manufacturing company Veloce was founded in 1905 by John Gutgemann, a German whose name was anglicised to Goodman when he was naturalised a few years later. Veloce was a family concern in which Goodman's sons, daughter and grandsons would come to play an important part. The company made a wide range of products, including bicycles and conventional 500cc motorcycles. When they decided to add a speedy lightweight two-stroke to the line-up, the name Velocette was chosen to suggest that it was a baby version of the bigger machines. In time the new baby became so popular that the company was named after it rather than the other way around.

Although beautifully engineered and commendably light, the frame and forks were conventional for the time, and the real interest lay in the engine and transmission. These were both very sophisticated for their day, and offered many advanced features.

The transmission was by chain throughout – at a time when many competitors relied on the much less reliable belt. It had the luxury of a two-speed gearbox, although no clutch was fitted. The gearchange was by a large knob looking something like a bathroom tap, fitted on the right of the tank.

Part of the reason for the absence of a clutch (in itself not uncommon for the period) was the crankcase design, which helped lead to the adoption of a very unconventional

Velocette Two-stroke (1922)

Years in production: 1915-22

Engine type: single-cylinder two-stroke

Bore and stroke: 67 x 73mm

Capacity: 220cc

Carburettor: Brown & Barlow two-lever

Tyres (front/rear): $2\frac{1}{4}$ x 24in/ $2\frac{1}{4}$ x 24in

Weight: 140lb

Top speed: 40mph

clutch on later models. The crankcase chosen was very compact and very narrow, contributing to a very stiff bottom end. On the early two-stroke, only one main bearing was used, and the crank was overhung. To balance it, the flywheel was fitted externally, and the drive chain ran inside this. A result of the narrow drive line is that the final drive chain is outside the primary sprocket, making the type of clutch adopted by most other designers an impossibility.

The benefit of the crankcase design was its strength, aided by a lubrication system that offered reliable oiling under all conditions. Most two-strokes then and for the next 50 years relied on hit-and-miss oiling by petroil lubrication. This was both messy and unreliable. Velocette offered a positive lubrication

system via a small container in the crankcase, which was automatically pressurised by the engine. This fed oil directly to the main bearing through an adjustable jet.

The top end was conventional for a two-stroke of the period, using a side-mounted induction tract and deflector-type piston to control the gas flow. Because of the absence of a clutch, a compression relief-valve was fitted to the front of the cylinder head to allow the engine to spin easily when starting off. In use the little Velocette was reliable and economical, while the absence of a clutch was no hardship at a time before heavy traffic existed. Light, simple and well-engineered, it paved the way for a company which would become one of the chief pioneers during the 1920s and 30s.

Triumph Ricardo

Having established an enviable reputation in the early days of motorcycle competition, Triumph chose to ignore events such as the Isle of Man TT for several years. So when they performed an abrupt about turn in 1922 it could be expected that they were pretty confident of the machine that they chose to enter – the super sports 'Ricardo'.

Sir Henry (Harry) Ricardo was a renowned combustion expert who had worked on behalf of many companies when he was asked by Triumph to advise on a replacement for their trusty side-valves. Ricardo produced a number of alternatives before Triumph announced that their new overhead-valve model would use a four-valve head design. In fact, from the cylinder barrel down, the rest of the machine was virtually identical to Triumph's tried-and-tested Model H side-valve – including cycle parts that were becoming dated by comparison with its rivals.

The theoretical advantages of a four-valve head were numerous. Gas flow could be more efficient, the spark plug could be positioned centrally for more efficient combustion, while the lighter components would respond quicker, allowing higher revs. In fact, Ricardo's design was quite conservative, using small ports and unusually recessed valves. Each pair of valves was parallel, set at 90 degrees to each other, with stems and springs exposed; the piston, which was of light alloy, had a concave crown and a slipper-type skirt. The cylinder barrel was made of solid steel and had very deep finning, while the head, which had two parallel exhaust ports, was iron. The valves were operated by rockers running in bearings carried in lugs cast into the top of the head. Two long, exposed pushrods ran up the outside of the engine.

Fully equipped for the road, the Ricardo was marketed as a super sports model, rather than a pure racer.

Triumph Model R (1923)

Years in production: 1921-28

Engine type: single-cylinder four-
valve ohv
four-stroke

Bore and stroke: 80.5 x 98mm
(changed to 85 x 88mm)

Capacity: 499cc

Power: 20bhp @ 4600rpm

Carburettor: Triumph twin barrel

Tyres (front/rear): 3 x 26in/3 x 26in

Transmission: Triumph
three-speed gearbox

Weight: 250lb

Top speed:
approx 70mph

From there down, the engine was based on the Model H. The flywheels were slightly smaller, to allow free revving, while the lubrication, relying on constant-loss fed by hand pump, was later changed to dry sump fed by external oil pump. The resulting Model R Fast Roadster was marketed as a fully equipped sports model and attracted favourable reports. In this form it lapped Brooklands at 68mph, having survived the test of a flat-out lap in first gear. A racing version with modified ports also took the hour record at almost 77mph, and a flying mile at nearly 84mph.

Three were entered for the 1921 TT, alongside a back-up team of side-valve Triumphs. Handling deficiencies of the standard Triumph forks meant that proprietary alternatives were substituted, but in this first foray only one finished, well behind its side-valve team-mate.

A year later, the Ricardo was back with the new lubrication system, stronger valve gear, a modified cylinder with new dimensions and made of cast iron, a three-speed gearbox and new front fork. This time, it finished second in the TT, and the following year went on to take a number of continental wins and gold medals in the ISDT.

After 1924, Triumph switched their development efforts to a new model, although the 'Riccy' stayed in their range as a sports model until 1928, when the looming Depression forced Triumph to reduce their range. But the four-valve layout had proved its potential, and in the hands of Rudge and others, in the future would go on to demonstrate its winning worth.

BSA Round Tank

For a long period in the interwar years the giant BSA conglomerate dominated a booming motorcycle market in a way that no other British factory could claim to have done. 'One in four is a BSA' was a factory advertising slogan, and it was no idle boast. Part of the reason why BSA became so big was that they understood the needs of the market. While their machines were far from the most glamorous – and for many years were never even involved in racing – they satisfied the demand for reliable, basic transport that even today underpins the exotic machines from the Japanese giants.

At one end of the market this meant heavyweight sloggers such as the BSA V-twins and 500cc singles, often seen pulling sidecars as family transport or workaday hacks. At the other end of the market it meant affordable lightweights and, in particular, 250cc singles, a market niche that BSA made very much their own. Their attack on this market began in 1924 and was very much a new departure for BSA. It was known to be a difficult market, for the public had been treated to many poorly designed and underengineered budget specials from other makers.

The little BSA Round Tank was a well loved utility machine that established its makers in this important market. Reliable and rugged, it put thousands of people on wheels and found favour with institutions as a hard-working despatch bike.

Perhaps as a result, the little BSA was solidly conventional, with a side-valve four-stroke engine in place of the often unreliable two-strokes usually offered. It was small and light and simple enough for a novice, while strong enough to take all that the most uncaring rider could throw at it. And it was cheap – less than £40. There was belt-and-braces lubrication, with a new-fangled mechanical pump as well as the old-fashioned hand pump, plus a sight feed to reassure the anxious owner that all was well. The oil was contained in the front section of the tank that gave the model its name. Handsomely finished, but rugged and simple like the rest of the machine, the oil tank was a simple cylinder with no weak seams to split, and was suspended within the frame by two simple metal straps.

Practical details abounded. The mudguards were surely some of the widest ever fitted to a motorcycle, genuinely capable of guarding against mud splashes in almost any conditions. Indeed, they were so wide that the front forks actually passed through them. All-chain drive was used, while the gearbox was operated directly by a long hand lever.

Ruggedness was such a concern of the factory that they boasted that the prototypes had been battered for hours on a special bumping machine to simulate years of heavy use. There were, of course, no breakages.

With such a concern for practicality it might seem odd that the factory chose not to fit a front brake. This was dictated by a feeling, dating back to pioneer days, that such a brake might be hazardous to the inexperienced rider, because of the risk of locking the wheel or skidding. It was felt that, with a modest top speed, a back brake should be perfectly adequate. In fact, BSA's design coincided with a new legal requirement that all machines should have two independent means of stopping. The factory solved that one simply by fitting two entirely separate systems to the back wheel. In addition to the footbrake, a friction block operated by the handlebar lever pressed on the dummy belt rim on the rear wheel.

The resulting machine was a pleasant utility bike that did a great deal to establish BSA's reputation for quality and reliability. One was even used in May 1924 as part of a BSA stunt, climbing Mount Snowdon in Wales in just over half an hour, alongside the mountain railway track. It sold in large numbers – some 35,000 – and was adopted by the Post Office for telegram delivery. This remained a familiar role for BSA lightweights for many years, right up to the era of the BSA Bantam and the twilight of a once-great British company.

BSA Round Tank (1924)

Years in production: 1924-27

Engine type: side-valve single-cylinder four-stroke

Capacity: 249cc

Bore and stroke: 63 x 80mm

Tyres: 24 x 2¼in beaded-edge type

Brakes: friction block on dummy belt rim (rear only – two independent systems)

Gear box: two-speed

Top speed: 43 mph

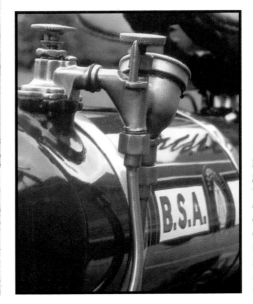

Suspended between the frame rails on two nickel-plated suspension bands, the tank that gave the model its name comprised a separate oil compartment in front of the main petrol tank. Rather unkindly, the machine was also dubbed the 'Flying Marrow'.

James V-twin

In their later years, when they were simply part of the giant AMC group, the name of James would come to be associated almost exclusively with the kind of budget two-strokes that represented the final fling of the British industry. But in the early days of the industry, the picture was very different, and the marque adopted the slogan 'The Famous James' for its twin-cylinder flagship.

The company had been founded in the late 1870s as a bicycle manufacturer, taking the name of founder Harold James. The James Cycle Company, based in Greet, Birmingham, soon grew to a substantial operation. It produced its first motorcycle in 1902. Like most other pioneer motorcycle experiments, the first James product was virtually a conventional pedal cycle modified to take an engine, with belt drive to the rear wheel. As well as this model, the company produced another version in which the engine drove a friction roller in contact with the rear tyre, an idea that was used in some cyclemotors of the 1950s.

The earliest James machines used proprietary engines, but within a few years the company was manufacturing its own two-stroke and four-stroke power units, as well as experimenting with advanced ideas such as drum brakes and quick-change wheels. The 1908 'Safety' model was influential on rival makers, and in 1911, James introduced a model with such 'modern' features as multi-plate clutch, a kick-start, two-speed gearbox and all-chain drive.

During World War I, James machines were used by the Allied forces, but a fire at the factory prevented them from going back into peacetime production immediately. The earliest postwar models produced were 250 and 350cc side-valve singles, and these were soon followed by popular V-twins of 500cc. An overhead-valve model was made as well as the side-valve version pictured here. Both included advanced features for the time and were a popular choice of the family man (with sidecar attached) and sporting rider.

Unusually, James made most of the components themselves, unlike the majority of factories which relied on many bought-in components. This included making the castings for parts such as the distinctive silencer box carrying the 'James' name cast into the side.

Popular as they were, the bigger James models were expensive to make and to buy. By the end of the 1920s, the Depression was starting to bite the motorcycle industry and James were able to buy up the ailing Baker company, makers of lightweight motorcycles. From about 1930, smaller machines powered by proprietary Villiers two-strokes became the mainstay of James' business, until they themselves were taken over after World War II.

The gearchange quadrant on the side of the tank (left) is a special alloy casting made in James' own foundry.

The carburettor (right), a Mills, is a forerunner of the later Villiers design. It uses a concentric float bowl and mixing chamber, unusual at the time, but later to become a common design feature.

James V-twin (1924)

Years in production: 1914–1932

Engine type: side-valve V-twin four-stroke (overhead-valve engine also manufactured)

Capacity: 496cc

Bore and stroke: 63x80mm

Compression ratio: 5.5:1

Carburettor: Mills

Transmission: all-chain, via three-speed gearbox

Top speed: 65mph

Resplendent in its green James livery, the 500cc side-valve model features the handsome alloy castings that were a factory trademark. Electric lighting was a luxury item for its day.

Brough Superior SS100

The Brough Superior has been called the first superbike. The aim of its designer George Brough was to build a machine that was the best at everything – the fastest, best looking, most advanced and best finished – and in its day the Brough Superior earned itself the title of the 'Rolls Royce of Motor Cycles'. The SS100 could top 100mph when half that speed was considered good going, looked like it cost a fortune – and did – and was the natural choice of the rich and famous.

George Brough's father William was a well-established motorcycle manufacturer who had built a range of reliable machines at his Nottingham factory since the 1890s. But George, an excellent competition rider, wanted something with more performance than the Brough product could offer. So in 1919, after failing to convince his father of the rightness of his ideas, son George set up his own works, also in Nottingham. The name, a friend's idea, was meant to suggest the bike was superior to everything else on the

road, but George's father could have been forgiven for taking it personally.

In fact almost every part of the Brough Superior was the product of another factory; engines mostly from the JAP factory in Tottenham, London, gearboxes by Sturmey-Archer, brakes from Enfield and so on. The forks were Harley-Davidson, later copied by Brough under their own 'Castle' trademark. But George Brough had chosen the best components available and put them together with a keen stylist's eye, to create something with a visual appeal that no other machine could better – and a performance to match. The earliest Brough Superiors had side-valve V-twin engines but were no slouches – 80mph being well within reach. The finish, with acres of nickel plate and enamel, was superb, and the tank, a Brough's crowning glory, was like no other.

George Brough was an excellent publicist, helping to sell the machines with his own exploits. In 1922 he rode his personal Brough Superior SS80, nicknamed 'Spit and Polish'

Brough Superior SS100 (1925)

Years in production: 1924-39

Engine type: 45 degree V-twin ohv four-stroke

Bore and stroke: 85.5x86mm

Capacity: 998 cc

Carburettors: Binks

Tyres (front/rear): 3 x 28in/3 x 28in

Wheelbase: 59½in

Weight: 330lb

Top speed: 100mph

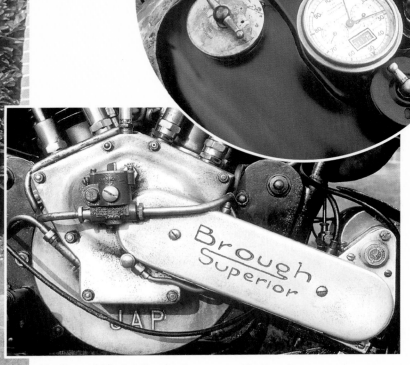

The distinctive, handsome Brough tank (right) carries filler caps for oil and petrol and a sight-gauge for the oil feed, as well as a handsome chronometric speedometer, then considered as an extra.

The featured bike is believed to be Lawrence of Arabia's fourth Brough. A 1925 SS100, it has exceeded 108mph. Supplied by Brough's London agent, it was fitted with several extras, including a specially modified tank, a toolbag and electric lights.

The Brough name on the magneto drive (above) only told part of the story, for the V-twin engine was the product of the JAP factory in Tottenham, as attested by the crankcase casting.

to win a Brooklands race at over 100mph, and took over 200 awards for his riding in trials and races. In 1922-3 he won 51 out of 52 sprints he entered – and the last was won by the bike without him, when he fell off forty yards from the finish!

In 1924 the first SS100 appeared. It had a 1000cc overhead-valve JAP V-twin engine and was based on the model on which rider Bert le Vack had taken the world speed record to 119mph. When launched, an SS100 cost between £150 and £170, according to specification – a huge sum when a modest house might cost £300 – but every model was guaranteed to have been tested at over 100mph and had handling to match, thanks to the excellent forks and frame. Sadly, the forks also led to the SS100's one weakness – the lack of a decent front brake. To add to the rider's comfort, the handlebars were made to suit the original owner, and many other options could be specified. Acetylene gas lights were the standard fitting on early

machines, as there was insufficient room for a dynamo, although later bikes came with electric lights.

Those who could afford it loved the SS100. One enthusiast was T E Lawrence, who as 'Lawrence of Arabia' had become a national hero. He owned seven Broughs in all – six of them SS100s – clocking up a total of over 300,000 miles and writing vividly about the excitement of his rides on 'Boanerges' (his nickname for his bikes).

The SS100 continued to be produced in small quantities, as befitted its high-quality status. In 1928 a long-stroke engine was introduced, which offered more power at the price of some flexibility. The JAP engine was redesigned in 1933 and in 1935 a Matchless engine was introduced. But in 1940, after two decades at the top, the Brough factory turned its production over to the war effort. When peace returned it ushered in a period of postwar austerity, and with no suitable engines being made, it was to be the end of Brough motorcycles.

Ner-a-car

The Ner-a-car was one of the most genuinely innovative 'motorcycles' ever made. A complete concept, it owed little to convention when it was designed, and embodied ideas that are still considered radical today. This makes it even more remarkable that in its day it was commercially successful enough to remain in production for some five years and sell in reasonable numbers.

Ner-a-car took its name from a double pun. Not only was it 'near a car' in its design principle, it was also the brainchild of an American called Carl Neracher. Working in a factory in Syracuse, New York State, Neracher built his first models in 1921, with the idea of making a machine that was more stable and comfortable than a conventional motorcycle could ever be.

The basis of the design was a low-slung platform of pressed steel, which housed the engine, transmission and rear wheel. Initially, there was no rear suspension, although this was later added. At the front, the frame splayed out to house the front wheel, which was suspended on coil springs and turned on a king-pin similar to a car's.

This form of hub-centre steering helped to make it possible for the machine to have an ultra-low centre of gravity and a more inherently precise control of steering and suspension. Its attraction is such that a similar principle has surfaced from time to time throughout motorcycle history, including on top of the range models from Yamaha and Bimota. Its chief drawback is the limited steering lock; in the case of the Ner-a-car leading to a turning circle of nearly 20 ft (over 6m).

This was a small price to pay for the machine's uncanny stability – such that it could easily be ridden hands-off – while with the huge front mudguard and wide footboards it offered excellent weather protection. The engine was under a cowling, which also helped to keep the rider clean. A later de-luxe model offered a windshield and instrument panel to give shielding as good as the best modern fairings.

At first, the power unit was a 211cc two-stroke single, and in this form the model was launched in Britain at the 1921 TT. The engine drove a large external flywheel, which also provided the unusual transmission. This consisted of a friction wheel in contact with the face of the flywheel, linked to the final drive sprocket, so that as the flywheel turned, it spun the friction wheel and hence the drive chain. A gear lever was used to track the friction wheel across the face of the flywheel, giving different gear ratios, while a twistgrip control could be used to disengage the friction wheel completely, acting as a clutch. The makers licensed the design to the British company Sheffield Simplex, who at first uprated the engine to 285cc. Later, to provide more power, they fitted 350cc side-valve and pushrod engines from proprietary makers Blackburne, together with a more conventional three-speed gearbox. The price of what had been an expensive machine came down, while Ner-a-car riders won an impressive number of awards in road trials.

It won customers who were a long way from conventional motorcyclists – much as the later scooters were to do – and by 1926 Sheffield-Simplex was catering to their needs with the de-luxe model's car-type seat and dashboard. Sadly, the market for such sophistication remained a limited one, and towards the end of the year production ceased for good.

Ner-a-car (1925)

Years in production: 1921-26

Engine type: single-cylinder side-valve four-stroke

Capacity: 350cc

Gearbox: Sturmey Archer three-speed

Wheelbase: 59in

Turning circle: 19ft 6in

Weight: 168lb

The front wheel is carried on a subframe suspended on coil springs. It turns on a swivel arm mounted in the hub.

Carburettor, crankcase and transmission (left) are normally concealed by a steel casing.

Incredibly low, the Ner-a-car's pressed steel frame encloses the crankcase and front wheel completely. The handlebars have a linkage to connect them to the steering.

Cotton TT

Built to prove a design principle, the vintage Cottons went on to win two 1920s TTs and score a further seven places – as well as launching the career of one of the greatest road racers in history.

Many engineers deplored the traditional motorcycle frame's dependence on inherently weak bent tubes, but few put their ideas into practice. Willoughby Cotton was a law student rather than an engineer, but he succeeded where so many others compromised. Before World War I he set out a principle of design in which all tubes were to be straight and fully triangulated. All tubes should be in compression or

tension, rather than subjected to bending forces. The design he sketched achieved all these objectives, with the secondary advantages that, as well as strength, it offered lightness and a low centre of gravity.

A prototype was constructed by Levis, but Cotton decided to go into manufacture in his own right. Abandoning his law career, he raised the capital to establish a factory in Gloucester shortly after the end of the war.

As a small factory, entering three machines in the 1922 Isle of Man TT was a bold stroke. Even bolder was offering a ride to an unknown Irishman aged just 17.

Cotton JAP TT (1927)

Years in production: 1927

Engine type: single cylinder overhead-valve JAP four-stroke

Bore and stroke: 85.5 x 85mm

Capacity: 490cc

Compression ratio: 6.5:1

Front forks: TT type

Gearbox: three-speed close-ratio

Weight: 285lb (approx)

The straight, triangulated tubes from headstock to rear wheel spindle were the principle on which Cotton was established, and are clearly visible on this 1927 500cc racer.

Stanley Woods was an aspiring racer without any real experience, who had written to every Senior TT manufacturer asserting that he already had a Junior (350cc) entry and now needed a machine for the Senior race. He had repeated this entirely fictitious claim in reverse for the Junior, backing up both claims with a largely fabricated testimonial. Cotton was the only marque that swallowed the fiction, although when Woods saw the tired old racer that they provided for the Junior, he reflected that maybe they had had the last laugh.

Despite enormous adversities, which included himself and the machine catching fire during refuelling, Woods rode a furious race to finish fifth, more than justifying Cotton's faith. The following year he stormed home to win ahead of a field that included the extremely competitive AJS and Douglas machines. Moving on to other marques, Woods would go on to win a total of 10 TTs, as well as a host of Grands Prix.

Cotton themselves continued to contest the TT throughout the 1920s, and in 1926 took all the first three places in the Lightweight (250cc) race. But such efforts always had to be supported by the manufacture of roadsters, powered by a wide variety of proprietary engines. After their popularity peaked towards the end of the 1920s, the Depression of the 1930s hit production badly and resulted in falling sales.

With the outbreak of World War II, motorcycle manufacture was curtailed and Cotton found themselves unable to diversify into other operations. They went into liquidation in 1940.

The firm was revived by new owners during the 1950s, as manufacturers of lightweight commuter machines. However these bore little relation to the original bike. In addition, their conventional frames were a far cry from the great design principle that had been laid down by the founder – one of the great innovators of chassis design.

The Cotton tank badge (right) reflected the triangulated principle of the frame, in which all the tubes were braced and subjected only to forces along their length.

Sunbeam Model 90

Such were the fine qualities of Sunbeam's roadster models that they were dubbed 'gentleman's motorcycles', but the Model 90, Sunbeam's most sporting machine of the 1920s, was more than capable of holding its own against all comers.

John Marston & Company, the firm that built Sunbeams, was founded in Wolverhampton, originally as makers of saucepans. In 1890 they began to make bicycles, which gained a reputation for fine finish and durability, as well as a practical chain enclosure – 'the little oilbath'. Marston's first motorcycle was built in 1912, and while conventional, was a sound design produced almost entirely in-house. The range expanded, and although Sunbeams were not cheap, they acquired a reputation for quality and reliability. After World War I, during which Sunbeams were used by the Russian and French forces, production of both singles and V-twin models continued.

The firm began entering reliability trials straight after the war, and re-entered racing soon afterwards. Riding side-valve 500cc machines, Tommy de la Hay won the 1920 TT with team-mate George Dance taking the lap record.

In 1922 Alec Bennett won again on a similar machine. Sunbeam had to wait until 1928 for another win, but this time it was their latest overhead-valve model ridden by the diminutive Charlie Dodson that secured them the honours.

Although the company had experimented with an overhead-cam design in 1925, the winning machine was effectively a works-prepared version of the catalogue Model 90 racer, itself similar to the Model 9 sporting roadster. To prove that his win was no fluke, Dodson repeated the performance in 1929, followed home by Alec Bennett on a similar machine. Many other wins were scored in continental Grands Prix, making the Model 90 effectively the last pushrod single-cylinder engine to be competitive in world class racing.

Early Model 90s followed the classic flat-tank styling and sported Sunbeam's renowned black and gold finish.

They were distinguished by their workmanship and immaculate finish, rather than the ingenuity of the design. The engineering was simple and solid, with long, hollow pushrods enclosed in separate tubes, exposed valves and twin exhaust ports for better cooling of the cast iron head. Large, well-balanced flywheels and a short, stiff con-rod characterised the bottom end, while the high compression piston and effective combustion chamber were the only secret of the top end. A close-ratio gearbox, racing cam profiles and hairpin valve springs were other distinctions between the Model 90 and its humbler brothers.

Dodson's own machines had to be specially adapted to suit his short stature, with lowered saddles and handlebars.

By 1929, when he won his second TT, a larger tank of the more fashionable saddle-tank design (and a modified frame) had been adopted, and a foot-change gearbox was used.

The Model 90 was made until 1933, and variants of the original design continued to be produced under differing model numbers until 1935, shortly before the company was taken over, and motorcycle production ceased with World War II.

Sunbeam Model 90 (1928)

Years in production: 1928-33

Engine type: single-cylinder ohv four-stroke

Bore and stroke: 80 x 90mm

Capacity: 499cc

Compression ratio: 7.5:1

Top speed: 90mph

The handsome chaincase (right), a Sunbeam speciality, is cast in light alloy. Twin exhaust ports were supposed to aid cooling.

GE 4768

1928 was the last year that the Model 90 used the flat-tank design. Holes drilled in the distinctive plate supporting the rockers are non-standard.

Velocette KTT

Throughout the 1920s the Velocette factory achieved a host of racing successes, thanks to innovative design and superlative engineering. The overhead-camshaft 'cammy' KTT models swept the board towards the end of the decade, particularly at the Isle of Man TT, which was then the most influential road race in the world.

Percy Goodman, the son of the founder, started work on a overhead-camshaft design as early as 1924 – when such ideas were extremely advanced. However, while it attracted much attention, the prototype was far from a success and

the model had to be heavily redesigned after its 1925 racing debut resulted in retirements.

This time, the design was an almost immediate winner, taking first place at the 1926 Junior (350cc) TT. In 1928 it became the first Junior machine to lap the Isle of Man at speeds of more than 70mph, and in total won eight TTs and Grands Prix.

From 1929 the KTT model was available to private owners as a 'race replica', which could be purchased for £80, and in private hands, cammy Velos went on to be the

The alloy casting (left) houses a pair of bevel gears driving the overhead-camshaft via the vertical shaft up the side of the cylinder barrel. Short rockers projecting from the cambox operate the exposed valves.

most successful amateur racing machines of the era, filling the first eight places at the Manx Grand Prix (the amateur version of the TT). By then a KTT had also put the world 350cc Hour Speed Record up to 100.39mph – the first time a 350 had topped 100mph. This feat was carried out at Brooklands by Velocette's own designer Harold Willis, one of the most innovative designers of his day and a brilliant development engineer.

In an era when cumbersome hand-change levers on the tank were the norm, the advantages of foot-change for racing had been recognised for some time. Several machines sported foot- or knee-change levers so that gears could be selected without letting go of the handlebars – but these were simply modified hand levers that had to be positioned exactly right for the chosen gear.

Willis devised the now virtually universal positive-stop gearbox, in which a single movement of the lever automatically selects the next gear up or down; the only limitation on the early KTT was that it retained a three-speed gearbox – changed to a four-speeder in 1932. The positive-stop gearchange was a brilliant innovation, which helped Velocette to become an even bigger success in competition and was immediately copied by most other manufacturers.

The 'K' series – a model letter that stood for camshaft – was developed throughout the 1930s, with variants such as the KSS (Super Sports) and KTS (Touring Sports). (TT of course meant TT replica.) Harold Willis even experimented with super-charging the works KTTs for two seasons.

Mass production of the KTT was discontinued in 1935, but the works racer continued to be developed. After reaching a peak just before World War II, the KTT series continued after the war with the MkVIII – itself to become a legend.

Velocette KTT (1929)

Years in production: 1925-50

Engine type: single-cylinder overhead-cam four stroke

Bore and stroke: 74 x 81mm

Capacity: 348cc

Compression ratio: 7.25:1

Power: 20bhp

Modified for racing, this KTT originally left the factory in July 1929 and was ridden to fourth place in the Manx Grand Prix that year. The rear subframe, a 1932 type, is a later modification.

Norton CS1

By the late 1920s racing had long been a main driving force of Norton's development, although the pace of technological change had accelerated rapidly. Until the beginning of the decade the main sporting effort had been carried by the firm's simple side-valvers, but in 1924 it was the new pushrod Model 18 that carried the factory to victory in the first TT since 1907. All that was about to change, for a scant three seasons later, the first of a long line of overhead-camshaft Nortons was to appear.

The CS1, standing for Camshaft One, was the brainchild of Walter Moore, a brilliant designer who had joined Norton

Norton CSI (1929)

Years in production: 1921-34

Engine type: single-cylinder side-valve four-stroke

Bore and stroke: 79 x 100mm

Capacity: 490cc

Compression ratio: 7:1

Power: 25bhp

Carburettor: Amal

Tyres (front/rear): 3¼ x 26in

Top speed: 85mph

Low-slung in the frame, the tall Norton CS1 engine set the tone for a generation of 'cammy' Nortons after it established its dominance in the 1927 TT.

The engine's clean lines and sturdy construction are typically Norton. But where on earlier models the crankcase itself linked the front and rear downtubes, engine and gearbox are carried above a forging that forms the bottom of a cradle frame. The three-speed gearbox has no positive stop, so gear selection requires very careful footwork.

long shaft housed in a tube running up the side of the barrel, splined to a second pair of bevel gears driving the overhead-camshaft. A pair of two-piece rocker arms projected from the camshaft housing to operate the exposed valves, which were returned by coil springs. The exhaust port was noticeably offset to the left to permit the smoothly curved exhaust pipe to clear the frame easily. The magneto was moved to the rear of the engine, with a diagonal chaincase fitted inside an extension to the chaincase on the left-hand side.

The new engine was fitted into the factory's full cradle frame, which now had a separate forging linking the front and rear tubes, housing the three-speed gearbox and the engine, where previously the crankcase had bolted directly to the front and rear tubes. Partly for this reason, the frame carried additional bracing stays to the rear wheel. Webb girder forks were fitted at the front, as was a large 8in diameter brake. A true saddle tank was fitted, concealing a frame that had to be tall, in order to accommodate the great height of the overhead-camshaft engine.

The new machines were ready for the 1927 TT, an event which they dominated in the hands of works riders Stanley Woods, Joe Craig and Alec Bennett. Woods led for much of the race and raised the lap record to over 70mph before retiring with a broken clutch. Bennett went on to win the race.

The next year a 348cc version appeared, and in 1929 was shown as the CJ, Junior model. Although there were few racing honours in either year, this was more a result of misfortune than the weakness of either the machines or the riders. The CS continued to demonstrate its superiority, and might have continued to do so for many years, were it not for the departure of its creator.

Walter Moore had accepted a lucrative offer from the German company NSU, for whom he would create a number of influential machines before he left with the outbreak of war. One of his first designs, however, was so closely based on the CS1, apart from using a four-speed gearbox, that the new 1930 NSU Rennmaschine was jokingly dubbed 'Norton Spares Used'. As Moore claimed the original design had been done in his own time, there was little that Norton could do to prevent him. They rapidly put together an alternative design, while Moore's NSUs were good enough to continue racing until 1935.

after stints at Douglas and ABC. Although he had been instrumental in developing the Model 18, Moore had long favoured the overhead-camshaft layout. After Velocette achieved a win in the 1926 Junior with their new 'cammy' model, and following rumours of other similar developments, Norton got the spur he needed. Taking up a design he had already sketched out, Moore laid down the machine that would carry Norton's works effort in 1927.

The bottom end closely followed the traditional Norton design, but cast into the side of the crankcase was a housing for the oil pump and a pair of bevel gears. These drove a

Scott Squirrel

Scott Squirrel (1928)

Years in production: 1926-40

Engine type: parallel twin-cylinder water-cooled two-stroke

Bore and stroke: 68.25 x 74.6mm

Capacity: 596cc

Carburettor: Binks

Gearbox: three-speed with hand change

Tyres front/rear: 3 x 20in/3 x 20in

Wheelbase: 55½in

Weight: 325lb

Top speed: 70mph

Scott built their reputation by flying in the face of convention. In the pioneer days, their delicate but never frail two-stroke twins were a delightful and effective alternative to the bicycle-framed, girder-forked, four-stroke single norm. But with the death of the founder in 1923 all that began to change. The late vintage Squirrel began a slow slide towards conformity that would eventually lose much of the charm of the originals. At the time, however, it seemed an attractive answer to satisfying the demands of an ever conservative mass market, and was a favourite machine for many competition riders.

The Squirrel name came into being in 1921, on the new 500cc sports model. It was an appropriate name for a cheeky, agile machine that was third in the Senior TT of 1922, made a fastest lap in the 1923 event and was second in 1924. At first, the Squirrel remained true to Alfred Scott's original open frame, two-speed concept. But from 1922, the company began to dabble with a three-speed design, using a conventional gearbox and clutch, and a three-speed

Handsome and more conventional in appearance than its predecessors, the three-speed Flying Squirrel suffered only from a thirst for fuel and a hefty price tag. Although the frame is still fully triangulated, the large fuel tank fills the centre of the frame.

Squirrel was shown in 1923. It was considerably more expensive than the two-speeder, and the company needed the income, for mounting debts forced an Official Receiver to take charge of the company.

Although the two-speed models remained in production until 1931, much of the development centred on the newer version. In 1926, the racing version's gearbox was much improved, but more importantly, the frame and forks were completely revamped. The frame was made of heavier tubing, and the fork was extensively braced. Although the frame was still triangulated, there was a top bracing tube, and the tank filled the open frame in a way that had already appeared on racing machines.

The desirable TT Replica of 1930 embodies racing features such as quick-action fillers and foot-change gearbox, but uses substantially the same mechanical design.

The resulting machine had a much more conventional appearance, but had gained around one-third in weight. Although the engine was also heavily revised, the extra power was scarcely in proportion to the change in power-to-weight ratio. Although the new Scotts made a poor showing in the 1926 TT, this model was the basis of the roadster Flying Squirrel models that followed. The 500cc machine that appeared at the 1926 Earls Court Show was effectively identical, along with a 600cc option. There was a considerable increase in price, making them around twice the price of a sporty four-stroke.

The year 1928 saw Scott's last place in a Senior TT, a third, and towards the end of the season the factory put a Replica on sale. It would become one of the best loved models. As part of a cost-cutting exercise for 1929, which saw the Squirrels drop in price, they also launched a more basic Tourer at under £70.

By 1931 Scott's financial straitjacket and the mounting recession had the firm in serious difficulties. There was no entry at the TT, nor the annual motorcycle show. There were detail modifications to the range each year, but the most

significant efforts were reserved for a prototype three-cylinder two-stroke. Although this was proudly shown in 1934, Scott lacked the resources to exploit the design.

The original Scott went out of production during the war and never really recovered after it. In 1950 the firm was sold to Matt Holder's Aerco company, based in Birmingham. Holder continued to sell bikes from the assets acquired, and it was not until 1956 that a new machine was built. The 'Birmingham Scotts' had a conventional swinging arm frame and a 600cc version of the Scott engine. Prototypes for variants were floated occasionally, but these came to little.

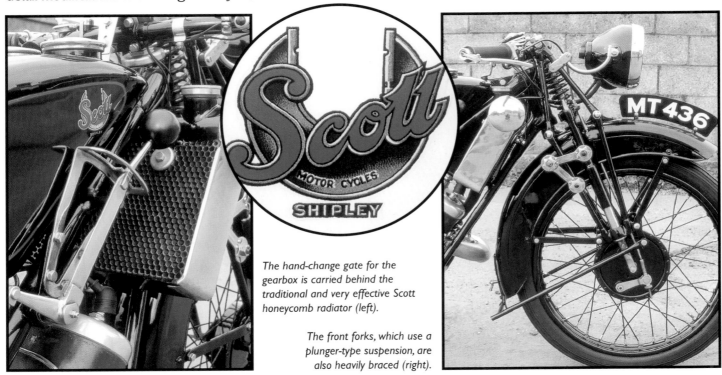

The hand-change gate for the gearbox is carried behind the traditional and very effective Scott honeycomb radiator (left).

The front forks, which use a plunger-type suspension, are also heavily braced (right).

Matchless Silver Hawk

The London-based Matchless company was among Britain's leading companies in the 1930s. Despite the depression it was sufficiently buoyant in 1931 to buy up the ailing AJS concern and merge it into Associated Motor Cycles Ltd (AMC).

In the autumn of the previous year, Matchless had demonstrated its buoyancy to an astonished public by launching an outstanding new model at the Earls Court Show. With a technical specification that reads more like the 1980s than the 1930s, the new machine was a 600cc four-cylinder design with overhead-camshaft, rear-sprung frame and coupled brakes, plus a stylish appearance and sporting performance.

Although its single-cylinder block made it hard to see the engine configuration, it was in fact a narrow-angle V-four. This was not the first time that Matchless had tried such a design – the company's earlier Silver Arrow had a similar layout. But the Silver Arrow had been a 400cc side-valve V-twin with two bores at an angle of 26 degrees to each other inside the single block. The engine was superbly quiet, but the model had been expensive and was too heavy to have a good performance. It also suffered from overheating, a side-valve trait aggravated by the substantial cylinder casting. It only remained in production for three years.

Designer Bert Collier, one of the two brothers behind Matchless, had decided to retain the best features of the Silver Arrow but give the sporting public the performance it craved. As on the Silver Arrow, the cylinder casting was in one piece, but this time there were four bores, with two

The instrument panel (above) was a practical feature borrowed from the earlier Silver Arrow.

pairs at the same 26 degrees to one another. The crankshaft ran across the frame, and the conrods were offset in two pairs so that the front and rear cylinders could be in line. Now that the valves were above the combustion chambers, it was possible to cast-in cooling air spaces between the cylinders. The overhead-camshaft and valve gear was driven by a shaft taken from one end of the crankshaft.

A single carburettor was fitted, with a cross-shaped induction tract that fed all four inlet valves, although in practice, gas delivery was far from even. The exhaust

Matchless Silver Hawk Model B (1934)

Years in production: 1931-35
Engine type: narrow-angle V-four overhead-cam four-stroke
Bore and stroke: 50.8 x 73mm
Capacity: 592cc
Gearbox: four-speed Sturmey-Archer
Top speed: 76mph

ports were coupled and a pair of exhaust pipes fed a single silencer.

The sporting 600 was fitted to a frame that was virtually the same as the Silver Arrow's. It included a rear fork pivoting on bonded rubber bushes, with a pair of springs and a friction damper under the single saddle. Handsome and stylish, the whole machine was designed very much in the current fashion and looked to have a bright future. The engine was so easy to start, it was said that it could be done by hand. Top speed was more than 80mph – very impressive for the time. The engine was flexible enough to potter along in top gear, an important consideration of the day when the awkwardness of hand-changing meant that riders liked to stay in top for as long as possible.

Sadly, just as with the Silver Arrow, there were overheating problems. The engine was hard to maintain, although it could be decoked in the frame. Other models suffered similar teething problems and overcame them through development – the Ariel Square Four, launched at the same time as the Silver Hawk, had its share of problems. But the Hawk proved just too expensive to survive more than five years, with not enough benefits to offer the limited number of customers who could afford it.

JU 4600

A handsome example of 1930's styling, the Matchless Silver Hawk had a lively performance and exotic specification that made it a star of the show when it was launched in 1930.

Excelsior Manxman

The Excelsior Manxman was one of the most successful products of the first company to build a British motorcycle. Excelsior was also to become one of the industry's last survivors.

Excelsior was founded in Coventry in 1874 as a bicycle manufacturer, but well before the turn of the century it had built Britain's first commercial motorcycle. During the pioneer years before World War I, the company produced small numbers of interesting machines, including an 850cc single, and was the first marque to achieve a mile-a-minute in a speed trial.

The firm was taken over by one of its suppliers after World War I, and the new management proved to be the spur to the firm becoming heavily involved in racing, as well as offering a range of everyday lightweight machines powered by proprietary JAP, Villiers or Blackburne engines. Their racing effort led to several successes – and when Excelsior's Syd Crabtree won the Lightweight TT in 1929, the firm offered replicas for sale the very next season.

Rather than rely on proprietary engines like so many others, Excelsior then decided to develop their own design, and in 1933 came up with a world beater. A 250, designed by Excelsior's Eric Walker and Blackburne's Ike Hatch, it followed Rudge's pioneering work on four-valve technology. Technically advanced but complicated, it used fully

Excelsior Manxman (1935)

Years in production: 1934-39

Engine type: single-cylinder single overhead-cam four-stroke

Bore and stroke: 63 x 69mm (250) 75 x 79mm (350)

Capacity: 249cc

Compression ratio: 6.5:1

Cylinder head: two-valve aluminium-bronze

Gearbox: three-speed close-ratio

Weight: 280lb

radial valves operated by pushrods driven from twin camshafts, and both inlet ports had their own carburettor. As Excelsior lacked their own engine building facilities, a small batch was built for them by Blackburne. Dubbed the 'Mechanical Marvel' this experimental engine won the 1933 Lightweight TT at a record speed in its first outing, despite atrocious weather.

The feat was not to be repeated, however, and in 1935 Walker and Hatch came up with a completely new design, the much more conventional Manxman, a two-valve machine using a bevel-driven single overhead-cam. Easier to build than the Mechanical Marvel, it was also very reliable and handled well, although it was rather heavy – perhaps as a result of being somewhat over-engineered.

The following year, as success still eluded Excelsior, the Manxman gained a four-valve head and took second place in both the 1936 and '37 Lightweight TTs, while a 350cc version scored a third in the 1937 Junior. More importantly for the company's fortunes, replicas were on sale to privateers, who kept the Manxman's name to the fore in racing for many years to come, while the model was also popular with sporting road riders.

At the TT, Excelsior continued to place each year until war brought an end to racing. In 1938, when they took second and third places, Excelsior used a spring frame, which added to the already good road-holding qualities. The performance was good enough to achieve Lightweight thirds in the first and second postwar events, but the company itself was not to return to the field in which it had once been so strong a contender.

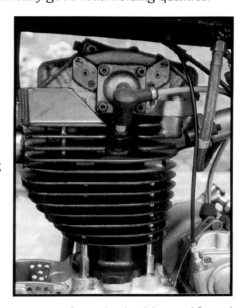

Bronze head, widely spaced fins and overhead-camshaft (above) are characteristic features of the Manxman.

A lightweight racer that was a little too heavy for ultimate success, the 250cc Excelsior Manxman was nevertheless a fitting tribute to Britain's oldest motorcycle manufacturer.

Norton International

Designed by development engineer Joe Craig in association with Arthur Carroll, the Model 30 appeared in 1930. The following year Norton achieved a host of wins around the world, so the name International was a natural choice for its premier racer. It had neatly trounced the opposition in the Senior TT, a feat repeated by the 350cc version in the Junior. In the autumn it took the one-hour record at Montlhéry at more than 110mph.

From 1932 the International that went on sale to the public was effectively a TT replica, equipped with road fittings – and many of the cycle parts were common to lesser models in the range with only minor modifications. The Roadholder forks were made by Norton in place of the Webbs fitted previously, and the frame was shorter and lower than the CS1 had used. Newly designed quickly-detachable wheels were a practical benefit of racing experience, while a large tank with sporting lines became an International hallmark and added greatly to the model's visual appeal.

Above all, it was the engine that defined the International. With a very strong bottom end and massive flywheels, the cylinder barrel and head were held down by long through bolts. The camshaft was housed in a completely separate casting that bolted to the top of the head. Long rockers protruded from slits in the cambox to operate the valves, the stems of which were completely exposed. The valve springs, originally coils, were changed to a hairpin type to allow rapid racing changes. A labyrinthine oil system fed lubricant to the big end, cylinder wall, cambox and valve guides via adjustable jets. Performance was in the 100mph region.

Minor improvements followed year-on-year. The forks and gearbox were redesigned in 1933 and from 1935 the gearbox was made by Norton

rather than Sturmey-Archer. From 1936 the racing specification included an alloy cylinder barrel and head with a bronze combustion chamber and aluminium fins.

The big change for 1938 was the adoption of plunger rear springing, as used on the 1937 works racers. By this time the Inter, sold with racing fittings, had begun to diverge widely from the standard sports models and had become very expensive. And from 1937, the true works racers had gained a double overhead-camshaft – the first step on the road to the evolution of the Manx Norton. But the Inter itself remained one of the most desirable motorcycles on offer, even if more urgent matters had begun to intrude. Production ceased in 1940 with the advent of war – the end of the first chapter in the International's story.

Tower of power (left): Norton's long-stroke single carries its valve gear in a separate casting bolted to the top of the cylinder head, resulting in a tall engine dominated by the polished tube housing the drive-shaft to the overhead-cam. The head and barrel are in cast-iron, but alloy was an option. While immensely tough, oil leaks from the cambox are a common feature of the design.

Norton International Model 30 (1936)

Years in production: 1931-39 (rigid) 1938-39

Engine type: single overhead-cam single-cylinder four-stroke

Bore and stroke: 79 ×100mm

Capacity: 490cc

Compression ratio: 7.23:1

Power: 29bhp

Carburettors: $1\frac{5}{32}$in Amal TT

Tyres (front/rear): 3 × 27/ $3\frac{1}{4}$ × 27in

Wheelbase: $54\frac{3}{4}$in

Top speed: 93mph

Girder forks and a rigid rear end are the hallmark of the early Inter. Two years after this model was made, Norton's newly developed plunger rear suspension was adopted, while postwar models gained telescopic forks.

Vincent Rapide

The Vincent motorcycle began and ended with an uncompromising vision: to be faster, more powerful, better at handling, and better all round than anything on the market. In many ways it succeeded, albeit at the cost of complexity and a price tag that put it out of reach of most customers. The ultimate form of the machine was very much the personal vision of the company's founder, Philip C Vincent. But it goes back even further than that, to another man with a personal view of what a motorcycle should be. This man was Howard R Davies.

Davies was a racer of no small ability, and won the 1921 500cc Senior TT on a 350 AJS. But becoming increasingly disillusioned with the failings of standard products, he founded his own company, HRD, in 1924. The bike was largely an assembly of proprietary parts – JAP engine, Druid or Webb racing forks, Burman gearbox – but he chose the best of everything, including larger brakes than most of the competition, and put them together with an expert's knowhow (and the aid of some capable designers). A low seating position and one of the first saddle tanks gave them a sleek appearance and good handling. In 1925 Davies proved his point by winning the Senior TT with one.

Always exclusive, HRDs sold in small quantities and foundered financially after just two years. The company and assets were bought by competitors OK Supreme. Enter PC Vincent. Educated at Harrow, Vincent had owned a 1923 BSA the defects of which so incensed him that he decided he could do better. Schoolboy sketches included a triangulated rear end with suspension units under the seat. Going on to study engineering at Cambridge, he built his first prototype while only 19 years old. It embodied those first ideas and attracted the attention of the influential editor of *The Motor Cycle*, who suggested that Vincent should purchase a known name, rather than try to attract the public with his radical ideas.

A proprietary JAP single-cylinder engine was a feature of the original HRD motorcycle. After Philip Vincent bought the name he continued for a time to fit these popular units, although now using a spring frame of his own design (below). Sales were slow at first, as the motorcycle looked complex and unconventional.

Few could argue with the phenomenal performance that resulted from the happy accident of the V-twin's design (right). Scarcely larger or heavier than a single it developed almost twice the power, while the spring frame gave the handling to cope with it and the twin front brakes provided the necessary stopping ability.

Vincent Rapide (1937)

Years in production: 1936-39
Engine type: 47.5 degree V-twin ohv four-stroke
Bore and stroke: 84 x 90mm
Capacity: 998cc
Compression ratio: 6.8:1
Power: 45bhp @ 5500rpm
Carburettors: $1\frac{1}{16}$in Amals
Tyres (front/rear): 3 x 20in/$3\frac{1}{2}$ x 19in
Wheelbase: 56in
Weight: 430lb
Top speed: 105+mph

Complexity became an art form in the shape of the Series A Rapide, dating from 1937 (left). The bike had a web of external oil pipes, which led to the model being dubbed a 'Plumber's Nightmare'.

Backed by his father, Vincent took over HRD's assets from OK Supreme in 1928. The factory was set up in Stevenage, north of London. The first products carried the HRD tank badge, but little else of Davies' designs remained. In place of the neat, stylish singles, Vincent's offerings looked complex. At their heart was a familiar JAP engine, but Vincent's triangulated spring frames were a far cry from the neat diamond familiar to most motorcyclists.

They were slow to sell, although matters improved after Vincent fell in with a young Australian engineer who was touring the world. Phil Irving would become his partner in making Vincent into a world beater. Supremely practical, Irving possessed the skill and vision to turn Vincent's ideals into a machine that looked sufficiently conventional to appeal to conservative riders, while giving it the performance that would turn heads.

Sales picked up in the early 1930s. In 1935 Vincent offered their own engine for the first time. A pushrod 500cc single, its most unusual feature was valves that were operated from the middle of the stem, supposedly decreasing wear and keeping the engine short.

The single began to gain enthusiastic followers, but in 1936 Vincent took the final step to legendary status. The turning point came when Irving noticed a drawing and a tracing of the 500cc Comet engine lying together. He realised that with few modifications a V-twin could be simply created, and that it would fit into the single's frame.

For little extra weight, the difference was phenomenal. Awesome power was available from the $47\frac{1}{2}$ degree twin, its angle an accident deriving from the necessity to line up the single's timing gear. The Series A Rapide could top 110. Some 80 were built before the war. After it, they would spawn one of the greats of the British industry.

Triumph Speed Twin 5T

The Speed Twin changed the face of motorcycling. Before it, most motorcycles, sporting or otherwise, were singles. But the Speed Twin was so immediately successful that almost all other factories jumped on the bandwagon with their own versions. Its parallel twin engine configuration was to endure until the demise of Triumph – and the industry – some four decades later.

One man can take most of the responsibility for the Speed Twin – Edward Turner, who had been the man behind Ariel's Square Four. Moving to Triumph, Turner quickly revitalised the firm's 250, 350 and 500cc singles as the Tiger 70, 80 and 90. Good looks and the exciting performance suggested by their name ensured the new models' popularity. However in 1938 Edward Turner brought out the range leader that would really put the Triumph company firmly back on the map.

There was nothing new about vertical twins – they had been tried by Triumph (among others) in the pioneer days, and again Turner's new Speed Twin was light and smaller than the Tiger 90, enabling it to slot into the same frame. Weighing 5lb less than the Tiger 90, it cost only £5 more at £75. At a glance, it even looked like a twin-port single, a distinct advantage in a notoriously conservative market. But it had better acceleration, pulled more smoothly and revved more freely, with valve gear many supposed to have been influenced by the sporting Riley cars.

The first Speed Twins had a one piece iron cylinder block with six studs holding the base. This proved a weakness and was soon changed to eight studs. The head was also cast iron. Camshafts in front and behind the crankcase opening drove pushrods between the cylinders, operating the valve gear in separate alloy boxes bolted to the head. Ignition and lighting were by a Lucas Magdyno fitted behind the cylinders, and lubrication was by double-plunger pump. Transmission was by a separate four-speed gearbox.

The appealing finish was Amaranth red and chrome with gold lining. The model looked clean and fast, and it was; delivering some 26bhp, the engine was good for around 90mph. In 1939 the factory produced a sports model, the Tiger 100, costing £5 more with a tuned engine, or £10 for an aluminium-bronze head. Finished in black instead of red, this model would top 100mph. Fitted with a supercharger, it took the Brooklands 500cc lap record to over 118mph.

Had it not been for the war, which soon interrupted production, the trend-setting Speed Twin

might have dominated the market even sooner. As it was, it ushered in a period during the 1950s when BSA, Norton and a host of marques such as Royal Enfield and Ariel all eagerly followed Triumph down a parallel twin route, which some detractors of the layout would call a blind alley.

Triumph Speed Twin 5T (1938)

Years in production: 1938-40

Engine type: 180 degree parallel twin ohv four-stroke

Bore and stroke: 63 x 80mm

Capacity: 498cc

Compression ratio: 7.2:1

Power: 27bhp @ 6300rpm

Carburettors: 1in Amal

Tyres (front/rear): 30 x 20/3¼ x 20in

Wheelbase: 55in

Top speed: 95mph

Looking almost like a contemporary twin-port single but with a much brisker performance, Triumph's handsome 5T was an instant hit.

BSA Gold Star

By 1937, BSA was Britain's largest motorcycle manufacturer, but it had built its reputation on providing good, solid workhorses, rather than racers. After a disastrous outing at the TT in 1921, BSA had turned its back on speed events, preferring to promote the product through reliability trials and other, off-road events.

So it was with some surprise that the Brooklands spectators noted the entry of a BSA 500cc Empire Star at a track meeting on 30 June 1937. Even more surprising was the rider, Walter 'Wal' Handley, one of the most accomplished racers of the day.

A sporting model introduced to mark the King's Silver Jubilee of 1935, the Empire Star had established a reputation for reliability and endurance, although with its iron-barrelled pushrod engine and heavy frame, it was not really considered a speed machine. But for 1937, designer Val Page had made major engine modifications, and the model had gained a new, much lighter frame.

In fact, Handley's mount was far from being a standard Empire Star. The riding position was adapted for racing, and the weight had been reduced. Inside the iron barrel it had a high compression piston suitable for alcohol fuel, and was fitted with a racing carburettor and magneto, plus special gearing. Races at Brooklands were run to a handicap, but even so, Handley stormed past the slower riders to lead from lap two. His fastest lap exceeded 107mph and he won the race at more than 102mph.

It was a long-standing Brooklands tradition that anyone who completed a lap at more than 100mph during a race was awarded a special enamel badge bearing a six-pointed star and the number 100 – the 'Gold Star'. It was no easy task to win one, and it was only natural that when BSA decided to capitalise on

BSA Gold Star (1939)

Years in production: 1938-39

Engine type: single-cylinder ohv four-stroke

Bore and stroke: 82 x 94mm

Capacity: 496cc

Compression ratio: 7.8:1

Power: 28bhp @ 5250rpm

Carburettor: Amal TT

Tyres (front/rear): 3 x 20in/ $3\frac{1}{2}$ x 19in

Wheelbase: 54in

Top speed: 92mph

Listed as 'the fastest standard sports machine' of its day, the BSA Gold Star represented a pinnacle of 1930s design and of pushrod engine technology. The frame had a conventional front fork and rigid rear, but nevertheless made a comfortable 90mph mount.

Based on the Brooklands trophy that gave the model its name, the BSA's Gold Star badge (above) dominates either side of the handsomely chromed fuel tank.

their success with the launch of a new sporting 500 in 1938, the tuned Empire Star would be called the Gold Star.

Listed as the model M24, the Gold Star was in fact substantially different from the machine that inspired it. For one thing, it had an aluminium head and barrel with cast-in pushrod tunnel, while the gearbox was cast in magnesium alloy. A racing Amal TT carburettor was used and a plain-barrelled silencer took the place of the Brooklands-can type that Brooklands racing regulations required. Engines were bench tested to give a guaranteed power output. Most of the rest of the machine followed the Empire Star, although both a trials version and a racer were also catalogued.

In fact, sales were poorer than might have been hoped, perhaps because the trend setting Triumph Speed Twin was launched at the same time as the Gold Star, while the new sports model was not as civilised as most BSA customers expected. But some competition success kept it in production and the next year a modified version appeared.

For 1939, the last year of production before the war, the gearbox had reverted to aluminium, and there were detail changes to the engine. Much more handsome in appearance, the new Gold Star was catalogued at £77/10/- as 'the fastest standard sports machine you can buy'. It was the beginning of a model that would become a legend.

Rudge Ulster

Rudge Whitworth's final sporting model was named after the race in which it won its greatest victory – the Ulster Grand Prix, billed as the world's fastest motorcycle road race. As it was first offered to the general public, the machine was virtually a race replica, although in later years roadster refinements were added.

Rider Graham Walker (later a journalist and father of motorsports commentator Murray) had been appointed Rudge sales manager in 1926. When he took first place in the 1928 Ulster Grand Prix, after an epic battle against rival Charlie Dodson on his Sunbeam Model 90, it was the first time a road race had been won at over 80mph. It was a win that had been eagerly expected – if Walker's Rudge had not suffered oiling problems on the last lap, he would almost certainly have won the Senior TT in the Isle of Man two months before, and the Ulster might have had another name.

Before the year was out, Ernie Nott took the world two-hour record at 100mph-plus, and there were further records in 1929. In Grand Prix racing, there were mixed

Rudge Ulster (1939)

Years in production: 1929-39

Engine type: single-cylinder, four-valve semi-radial ohv four-stroke

Bore and stroke: 85 x 88mm

Capacity: 499cc

Compression ratio: 7.25:1

Brakes: 8in coupled, front and rear

Power: 45bhp @ 5300rpm

Carburettors: $1\frac{1}{16}$in Amals

Tyres (front/rear): $2\frac{3}{4}$ x 21in/ $2\frac{3}{4}$ x 20in

Top speed: 85mph

The clean lines of Rudge's top sporting roadster – as well as its four-valve engine – derive directly from the machines that won the Ulster Grand Prix and many other races of the 1930s.

fortunes until 1930, when the first two Senior TT and the first three Junior places all fell to Rudge.

The winning formula was a triumph of technology and engineering. For years, Rudge had championed the four-valve head as the means to improved combustion efficiency and power. The 500cc models used a pent-roof head design, with two pairs of valves operating on parallel slopes like a pitched roof. The 350cc Junior version used a more complex radial-valve layout with all four valves angled in to the hemispherical combustion chamber. An efficient four-speed gearbox and massive drum brakes which were a byword for power helped the rider to make the most of the engine performance.

All three 1930 Junior Rudges were home at more than 70 mph, the first machines to break this barrier. It was the last year in which a pushrod machine would win the race, although the Lightweight TT fell to the 250cc version in 1931. As late as 1934, a trio of 250s privately entered by Graham Walker scored a Lightweight hat trick.

The 1931 (below) Ulster, shown in racing trim, is small and lithe with a leaner look than the later machine.

As a result of the factory's racing achievements, the range-leading Sports models were rechristened the Ulster in 1929. Refinements included dry-sump lubrication, a new crankcase and enclosed valves. Later models acquired contemporary styling, while the performance kept pace with the times – a claimed 100mph in 1930.

Financial troubles were a constant factor for Rudge. The years 1931 and 1932 saw very poor sales, and in 1933 the company had to halt many of its development projects, as well as giving up racing –although private entries continued throughout the 1930s.

Later that year, Rudge went into receivership, but this was not to be the end, and in 1936 the music and electrical company EMI, a major creditor, took over Rudge. One of the first developments to affect the Ulster and Special model was a new aluminium cylinder head with enclosed valves and revised oiling. During 1937 the factory was moved to EMI's base at Hayes, Middlesex. Sales gradually improved, but it was not enough to save Rudge. With the outbreak of war, EMI had to concentrate on its main business, chiefly the assembly of radio and rader equipment. Although they had intended to resume production when peace came, this was not to be, and in 1943 the Rudge name and tooling were sold off to Raleigh – a sad end to a great pioneering marque.

Manufacturers' badges from 1920–1939

The Classic Era

1940-1960

BSA M20 ✪ Excelsior Welbike ✪ AJS 7R

Triumph GP & Trophy ✪ Vincent Rapide ✪ Velocette KTT

LE Velocette ✪ BSA Bantam ✪ Norton Model 18 & ES2

BSA A10 Golden Flash ✪ Royal Enfield Bullet ✪ Sunbeam S8

Vincent Black Prince ✪ Ariel Square Four ✪ Douglas Dragonfly

Norton Dominator ✪ Velocette MSS ✪ Norton International

BSA Gold Star ✪ Triumph Tiger Cub ✪ Panther M120

The Classic Era

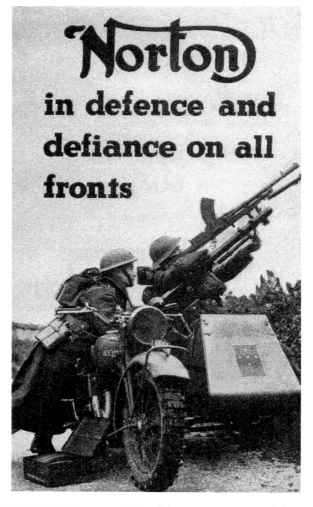

Norton in defence and defiance on all fronts

World War II meant the end of one era and the beginning of another. Economically, it would sap Britain's reserves and precipitate the break-up of an Empire that had once formed a captive market for British goods, and a cheap source of raw materials. It would also give wider horizons to a postwar generation. But first, there was the reality of a conflict in which every available resource had to be mobilised.

Of course this included the motorcycle industry, although not necessarily in the production of motorcycles. Some of Britain's most prestigious names ceased production and were turned over to making precision parts for other industries, or machines that were more suited to the war effort. For the big firms, motorcycle production did continue, for the most part, although on a severely restricted basis. Most manufacturers had been attempting to interest the War Office in the machines they thought most suitable, but in the event the military fell back on the tried-and-tested. BSA produced a stream of 500cc side-valves, the M20, while Norton turned out vast quantities of the similar 16H. Matchless produced the most forward looking of the machines built in quantity, the lightweight 350cc overhead-valve G3, which, when it gained 'Teledraulic' telescopic forks, became a forces favourite.

Of the major makers, only Triumph was not largely involved in wartime production. They would have been, had it not been for the Coventry blitz, which destroyed their factory early in the conflict. Other factories made machines in smaller numbers, including the specialised lightweight folding bikes from Royal Enfield and Excelsior, designed to be landed with paratroops. Norton made a Big Four-powered sidecar outfit designed as a gun platform, adopting an ingenious sidecar wheel

Wartime innovations tended to concentrate on the specialised. Norton's Big Four driven-wheel sidecar outfit (above) was capable of impressive off-road performance, but was deemed so hazardous to drive under ordinary conditions that the sidecar wheel drive had to be removed before any were sold off as Army surplus

On active service (left): the military motorcycle, typified by BSA's M20 and Norton's 16H side-valve performed essential service in many theatres of war. But although wartime proved the technical spur for advances in aviation and other fields, most service bikes were based on worthy but basic prewar designs.

In the immediate postwar period there was a massive demand for transport, yet motorcycles and the petrol to power them were both in short supply. Autocycles, precursors of the modern moped, provided one answer.

drive to enable it to negotiate rough terrain, and there were many other weird and wonderful offerings that failed to get into production.

Although Germany made great use of BMW sidecar outfits and lightweight solos in their 'lightning war' tactics, in the end the main use of the Allied military machines was, as in World War I, as despatch and convoy escorts. Over 400,000 British WD bikes were made, and thousands of riders were trained to use them.

When peace returned, as in World War I there was an immediate demand for transport. This time, there were many more experienced riders who were hungry for machines, and as before the demand was met with a mixture of reconditioned ex-service bikes, secondhand machines and finally a trickle of new models.

Again echoing a previous conflict, there were numerous shortages. Many materials were in short supply, but the chief disadvantage for the ordinary rider was the rationing of petrol. Supplies of a low octane, unbranded 'Pool' petrol began in mid 1945, but private owners were restricted to three gallons a week, or two for machines under 250cc.

New models were not long in coming. Triumph, courtesy of a new factory, was first in production with a postwar range of parallel twins. BSA and AMC rapidly followed suit, although it would be a long time before any of the returning servicemen and women could aspire to anything so exotic. For many, the route on to two wheels was via an autocycle, forerunner of the moped, or even a bicycle assisted by a clip-on motor.

The prewar depression had seen declining numbers of machines on the road from an all-time high in 1929, but within a year of peace there were half a million bikes in use – nearly double the 1939 total. All this despite an 'export or die' policy imposed to pay off crippling war debts, which meant most of the new machines produced went overseas. Machines had also become more expensive, thanks in part to the new purchase tax imposed during the war.

As a result the machines that most people were riding were extremely basic and in a low state of tune. Wartime experience had made most machines reliable, but many of the commonest conveniences were still considered extras – items such as pillion seats and footrests, air filters and speedometers. And despite the Brave New World promised by makers such as Triumph, most of the 'new' models on the market were warmed-over 1930s designs, dependent on worn tooling in factories that had seen only limited investment for years.

The mood, though, was one of optimism. There were bright ideas aplenty, including some, such as BSA's Bantam and Sunbeam's S7, that were copied from, or inspired by, successful enemy designs. Competition riding had returned

Despite postwar austerity, there was still room for the superlative, such as the Vincent Black Shadow, amply able to boast that it was the world's fastest, and prove it, time and again.

Motorcycle production boomed throughout the 1950s, buoyed up by an eager home market and healthy export business.

as early as June 1945. At the same time, a new movement was under way, with the formation in 1946 of the Vintage Motorcycle Club to ensure that older machines were valued and preserved. Major competitions began to return that year with the first postwar Manx Grand Prix.

The winner of the Senior race proved prophetic. Ernie Lyons was mounted on a new Triumph twin, with a specially developed alloy engine. Over the next few years the type would become the staple diet of the British industry, with BSA, Norton, AJS, Matchless, Ariel, Royal Enfield and others offering their alternative parallel twins.

TT racing returned the next year, although shortages of raw materials meant the cancellation of the planned industry show. Many of the technical improvements of the prewar racers had centred around supercharging. Such 'artificial aids' were now banned by the sport's organising bodies and, as a result, several of the British industry's most promising designs lost their advantage. Postwar racing tended to centre on the single-cylinder overhead-cam Manx Norton, with similar offerings from AMC and Velocette making up the field. Occasional exotic designs such as the AJS 'Porcupine' surfaced, but despite the undoubted success of the singles, there was little with a technology that could challenge the four-cylinder Italian racers soon being fielded by Gilera, or the technically advanced Moto Guzzi singles.

As the 1940s turned into the 1950s, things still looked good, however. The British industry was booming, with exports at record levels. British bikes were winning races and setting records, with machines such as the exclusive Vincent twins setting the standard by which all others were judged.

There were still shortages, however. With petrol supplies settling down, the Korean War meant that chroming had to be restricted, resulting in a couple of years of painted rims and other items. And behind the scenes the British factories were suffering from a shortage of real investment.

The German factories, starting for the most part from scratch, were coming out of a period of restricted production with machines that formed the basis for their own postwar expansion, as well as the model for Japan to do the same. Italy was offering a host of new ideas, including the scooter. The Vespa, launched in 1946, would spawn a European boom in which any British offerings were too little, too late. Owing little or nothing to anything that had gone before, or motorcycle convention in general, the Italian scooter was poorly understood and all-too-easily dismissed in Britain.

Many famous names failed to reappear after the war and many succumbed soon after it, including Douglas, which soldiered on for a scant 10 years. Despite the attraction of models such as the much-prized 90 Plus, chronic under-investment would eventually prove the downfall of the company.

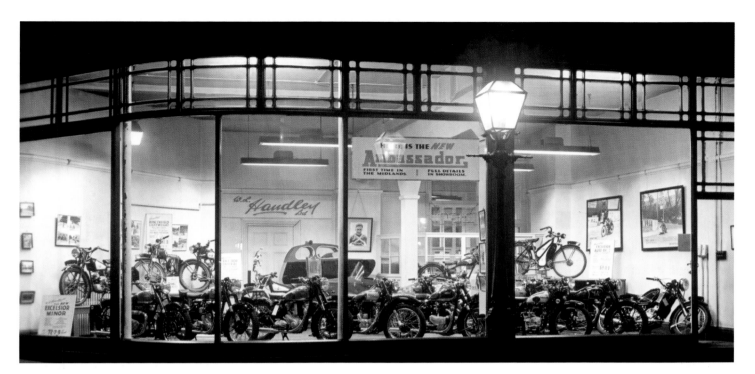

Throughout the 1950s, motorcycle dealerships could still afford to be exclusively British. The Birmingham showrooms of prewar racer Wal Handley offered a range of machines from Ariel, BSA, Excelsior, Matchless, Royal Enfield, Scott and Triumph, as well as the new offering from Ambassador, the postwar concern started by ex-racing driver Kaye Don.

This was caused in part to sales that were booming without the need to adopt such foreign ideas. In 1953, motorcycles topped the million mark, and Prime Minister Harold Macmillan's vision of a Britain that had 'never had it so good' was entirely believable. Britain was the largest motorcycle producer outside the Iron Curtain countries, and in a position to dictate its own terms.

Several motorcycle manufacturers had their own ideas of a Utopian machine that would provide transport for the masses. Velocette offered the LE and Ariel the Leader, in both cases backing their hunches with massive investment, which would prove ill-judged despite the clear advantages of the machines themselves. More conventionally, Norton had a frame, the Featherbed – even if, strictly, it had been developed independently in Ireland – and suspension that would set the standard for years to come. However, this would in itself mask for a few years the advances in engineering design that had been made by the continental opposition, and not just in the field of racing.

This was not to say that British machines did not still lead the world. One only had to look at the competitive records achieved by machines such as the Triumph twins, BSA's Gold Star, the Manx Norton, the AJS 7R and the racing Velocettes to see that, while machines such as the Vincent were still offering a performance that no rivals could match. But there were also external factors that were affecting the market for the British industry's products. In the early 1950s motorcycles were still everyday transport, for prosperity had still not improved to the degree where cars were affordable by the mass market. Lightweights provided commuters with a ride to work, while larger models suited the sporting rider or sidecar user. Sidecars were still commonplace family vehicles. But all this was changing, and at a pace that was too fast for most of the British industry to perceive.

Light cars such as the Mini were under development, at a price that would soon challenge the family sidecar outfit, while offering their owners far greater convenience. The Italian racing bikes, which started to demonstrate their technical superiority in the mid 1950s, had now espoused streamlining, offering still greater speed potential. Sales of two-wheelers were going up, it was true, but many of them were scooters.

By the end of the decade motorcycle sales had reached a peak that had not been seen for 30 years. But in truth there were troubles behind the scenes throughout Europe. The Italian companies that dominated road racing – Moto Guzzi, Mondial and Gilera – had withdrawn, in part as a result of the high costs. German factories were closing as the economic pendulum swung back in favour of the light car. And in Britain the image of the motorcycle, as well as its economic position, was altering fast.

What had been accepted as family transport a decade before was now increasingly associated with the youth market, and at that, the undesirable 'coffee-bar cowboys' who had latched on to the image of the motorcycle outlaw portrayed in the banned 1953 film *The Wild One*. Softened and detuned, this provided a model for suburban rebellion across Britain. With the ready availability of relatively cheap, fast and raw machines from all the British factories, the scene was set for a major shift in public attitudes to motorcycling.

Technologically, things were also changing fast. It was prophetic that while the last TT of the 1950s was dominated by the Italian MVs and the British Nortons, that year's competition also saw the debut of a new name – Honda – and a new challenge to British industry.

BSA M20

When World War II began, BSA was Britain's major motorcycle factory, with the proud boast that 'one in four is a BSA'. The firm had supplied the armed forces in World War I, and as befitted a company that began as an armament manufacturer, had geared up to produce munitions as early as 1935. They would go on to become the biggest supplier of motorcycles to the forces, in the somewhat unlikely form of their model M20.

Originally launched in 1937, mainly as a sidecar model, the M20 used a 500cc side-valve engine in a heavy frame. BSA had been supplying the War Office with a variety of models for evaluation, and in some cases purchase, since the late 1920s. But following the failure of their 1935 submission, the 35-6, the company submitted the M20 in 1936, only to see this fail, too, owing to heavy engine wear. Resubmitted the next year, it passed, but only marginally, and a small batch was purchased in 1938.

The War Office then issued specifications for a lightweight model, specially designed for service use, and BSA, along with the other major manufacturers, developed their own prototype. Although this was well received and a few were built, the official policy then changed to favour the machines that were already in service, whose reliability was well known, principally the Norton 16H and M20. Large quantities of the BSA model were purchased, until it eventually became the leading service model, although far from the most popular with its riders.

Heavy, bulky, slow and with limited ground clearance, the M20 had far from an ideal specification, but it was rugged, generally reliable and easily repaired. Special fittings included a long, spiked prop stand for field use and a large headlamp, fitted with a blackout mask in many areas of operation. There were other detail changes up to 1942, when shortage of rubber led to the replacement of rubber items such as hand grips with canvas fittings and footrests with simple metal ribs. A large air filter mounted on the tank and coupled to the carburettor by a hose was fitted for use in dusty climates such as the African desert. As a result part of the rear of the tank had to be cut away.

Comprising details from various years between 1940-42, this BSA M20 is typical of WD models that were rebuilt many times, losing their original identity in the process. The rear frames for canvas panniers are a standard military fitting.

The M20 used BSA's heavyweight girder forks (left), here liberally finished in khaki paint like the rest of the machine.

BSA M20 (1940)

Years in production: 1937-55

Engine type: single-cylinder side-valve four-stroke

Bore and stroke: 82 x 94mm

Capacity: 469cc

Compression ratio: 4:9:1

Power: 13bhp @ 4200rpm

Top speed: 60mph

Simplicity itself, the M20's rugged side-valve engine had massive flywheels, a low compression ratio and soft valve-timing which made it both forgiving and flexible, with plenty of low-down torque, coupled to a standard BSA gearbox. The primary drive chaincase was a sheet steel pressing secured by a host of small screws, but the exposed rear chain had to take its chances in the desert sand or northern mud.

Purchased for despatch and escort duty, the M20 served in many theatres of war. Over 125,000 were purchased by the armed forces. Finish consisted largely of applying khaki paint liberally, often including the engine,

tyres and even the saddle, with different camouflage schemes in various countries.

Vast numbers of M20s were discharged at the end of hostilities, and after gaining a new coat of paint were snapped up by a transport-hungry public. However the model stayed in service in smaller numbers for many years – in some cases as late as 1971. The vast quantities built mean that ex-WD M20s are still in use in many parts of the world, and it is even possible to find that new spares are still available. The civilian model was manufactured until 1955, with its 600cc cousin the M21 soldiering on until 1963, the last side-valve built in Britain.

Excelsior Welbike

The Excelsior Welbike was an ingenious oddity that grew out of the special needs of wartime. Intended to be dropped by parachute or landed by glider as front line transport for the Airborne Forces, the machine had to be cheap, lightweight, small and expendable.

The motorcycle to fit the bill was not designed by the Excelsior factory themselves. A long established engineering concern, Excelsior could lay claim to being the first British maker of motorcycles for sale to the general public, but was never a major manufacturer. In fact, at the beginning of the war the factory undertook contract engineering rather than motorcycle production.

Instead, the prototype was produced at the government's military research centre in Welwyn in Hertfordshire – the reason for it being named the *Wel*-bike. Its designer, a Mr. Dolphin, began with a standard airborne equipment container and sketched a miniature motorcycle with handlebars and saddle that folded to fit inside. Powered by a 98cc two-stroke Villiers autocycle engine, the result was crude, but tough and effective. There was no suspension, no lights and only one brake, the bare minimum necessary. The tiny fuel tank had to be pressurised by pump as it was too low to supply petrol by gravity feed – but this could be done before it went into action. To ready the Welbike for use, the handlebars simply had to be swung up and outwards until they locked on spring-loaded pins. The saddle was then pulled up and the footrests pushed down until they locked.

1943: a paratrooper unpacks the lightweight Welbike, which has been dropped in the special container shown.

An early Welbike with 98cc Villiers autocycle engine. Rubber shortages led to the use of brass and canvas handlebar grips seen here. Also clearly visible is the pump for pressurising the fuel tank.

Excelsior was contracted to build the machine, and after some refinements it went into production with Excelsior's own 98cc autocycle engine. As planned, the Welbike could be made very cheaply and quickly – so quickly that frame, engine and all were painted in one go while still on the production line.

Almost 4000 were built and saw action in parachute drops as well as beach assaults from 1942 until the end of the war. The bike's use, however, was limited by its low performance, especially over rough terrain. In the heat of battle, even the few seconds needed to remove it from its container and unfold it were seen as a drawback. As a result many saw more use as airfield transport than on the front line.

After the war some were sold off – although, without fitting a front brake, they could not legally be used on British roads. Meanwhile the original designer had been developing a civilian version, which he showed to the general engineering concern Brockhouse Engineering just after the war. Brockhouse built the model in small numbers and sold it as the Corgi, using the single-speed Excelsior engine. It soon proved to be too slow and too unrefined even for a transport-hungry postwar economy, and was soon discontinued – although the concept returned in a much more sophisticated form with the folding Honda 'monkey bikes' of the 1960s and 70s.

Meanwhile Excelsior continued production of their own autocycle and later built a popular two-stroke 250cc twin, the Talisman. The firm survives today as the makers of Britax accessories.

Excelsior Welbike (1942)

Frame: twin loop tubular with folding handlebar and telescopic seat tube

Suspension: none

Gearbox: none – single speed

Engine type: two-stroke, petroil lubricated

Capacity: 98 cc

Ignition: flywheel magneto

Lighting (on Corgi): 6 volt dynamo in flywheel magneto

Wheels: 10in, 20 psi front, 35 psi rear

AJS 7R

Known as the 'Boy Racer', the 350cc AJS 7R was one of the most successful club racing machines of its time – dominating the amateur Manx Grand Prix for many years. It is directly related to the 500cc Matchless G50 that came to be a major force in classic racing decades later.

Well before World War II AJS had successfully developed the R7 model, which used a tensioned chain drive to its overhead-camshaft. Although the firm had been absorbed by Matchless and become part of Associated Motorcycles Ltd (AMC), when the 7R appeared in 1948 it bore significant similarities to the earlier design. Although it was accused of being a copy of Velocette's KTT model, sharing the Velo's dimensions, the valve drive was again by chain, rather than shaft as on the KTT, and the 7R had a much more modern frame with welded construction and telescopic fork – AMC had pioneered the use of such technology with the much-copied wartime Teledraulic fork. Many castings were in light alloy, including magnesium, which was used extensively. As a result the 7R was much lighter than the KTT, and looked altogether like a postwar design rather than an update of a prewar machine.

The year 1948 was not perhaps the best time to launch a performance machine, for the low-octane petrol restriction of the time stifled performance. It was four years before the

7R demonstrated the force that it would become, with a win in the 1952 Junior (350cc) Manx Grand Prix by rider Bob McIntyre, who trumped this with a seond place in the 500cc race the same year.

AJS development engineer Jack Williams then took a hand, using early gas flow experiments to help develop a more efficient head design, together with an improved cam and valve setup. These ultimately took the power up by nearly 15 per cent, while the weight also went down by some 8 per cent by late 1954, turning the machine into a potent racing force.

The distinctive gold-finished chaincase (right) for the drive to the overhead-camshaft, was fitted with a Weller blade tensioner.

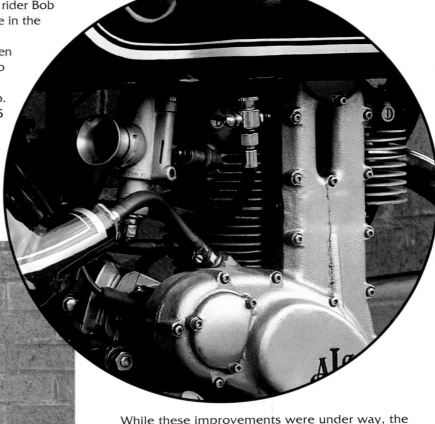

While these improvements were under way, the works was also developing an experimental model using three valves (a single inlet and twin exhausts) designed in 1952 by Ike Hatch. The idea was to improve cooling and allow the sparking plug to be placed in the theoretically better central position. The earliest version used a modified version of the normal AJS chain-driven overhead-cam. A later version improved the power output – however, the complexity of the redesigned valve gear meant that the drive had to be by shaft rather than the normal chain.

In a record breaking attempt later that year at the banked Monthléry track near Paris, the three-valve AJS machine took a total of five world records. Two years later, in 1954, the development team's efforts paid off when rider Rod Coleman won the Junior TT, followed home by D Farrant, thus ending a period of four straight Norton wins. Unfortunately the works abandoned the development of this machine soon after, leaving the successful two-valve to soldier on as the mainstay of a racing effort that sustained hundreds of privateers long after the factory itself had ceased production.

In traditional black and gold finish, the AJS 7R was the epitome of the British postwar club racing single. The factory development went on to win a TT, while countless amateurs achieved personal triumphs.

AJS 7R (1948)

Years in production: 1948-54

Engine type: single-cylinder single overhead-cam four-stroke

Bore and stroke: 74 x 81mm

Capacity: 348cc

Compression ratio: 10.8-12.2:1

Power: 37bhp @ 7500rpm – 42bhp @ 7800rpm

Weight: 285lb

Top speed: 102mph

Triumph GP and Trophy

Before World War II, Triumph had laid the foundation of the sporting parallel twin with its ground-breaking Speed Twin. A decade later, the company's racing machines showed the high-speed potential of the format and helped to confirm the postwar popularity of the format.

Triumph might have been expected to play a major part in the war, but the bombing raids on Coventry so damaged the factory that it was only able to resume limited production during 1942 at temporary premises in Warwickshire. Triumph intended to concentrate its military production on a 350cc machine based on the Speed Twin, but in fact the only model built in quantity was a 350cc single. Something that was to have more postwar relevance was not a motorcycle at all, but an auxiliary generator unit built for the Air Ministry. This used a lightweight, all-alloy version of the twin engine with ducted cooling, coupled to a direct current generator.

Production of the Speed Twin and Tiger 100 resumed in 1945, and these models were soon modernised with telescopic forks. It was shortly afterwards that Triumph staff realised that the leftover stock of cylinder barrels from the

generator unit offered the potential to create a lightweight, high-performance version of the Tiger 100. In particular, they provided a means of curing the overheating, to which highly tuned Triumph twins were prone.

Prototypes were prepared by Freddie Clarke, a prewar record-breaker, and one was entered in the 1946 Manx Grand Prix, ridden by Ernie Lyons. The model achieved a famous win ahead of the second-place Manx Norton, but it was said that managing director Edward Turner, who was opposed to racing, was not pleased that the model had been developed in his absence and without his approval.

Nevertheless, the race-prepared machine produced between 25 and 30 per cent more power than the sports roadster, and went into limited production. The generator-based engine was housed in a basically rigid frame fitted

Triumph's first postwar racing twin won the Manx Grand Prix in 1946. This is a 1948 model, with the all-alloy engine based on the wartime generator, racing megaphone silencers and sprung-hub rear suspension.

with Triumph's telescopic fork. A form of rear springing was offered by the Turner-designed sprung-hub. This comprised a large drum, inside which was a plunger springing unit. Although it could be fitted to a rigid frame without modification, the sprung-hub provided a limited degree of movement and was also prone to rapid wear, which could result in severe handling problems.

Despite this, in 1948 the GP model, as it was called, won the Manx Grand Prix again, and over the next few years made its mark in road racing. It was phased out in 1950, making way for race-kitted versions of the T100, but it had already become part of the Triumph legend.

There was another side to the story. In 1948 Triumph had entered an official team in the International Six Days' Trial in Italy, and had created three special machines. Again they had used the light alloy cylinder barrels, again they were based on the roadster twins. Sweeping all before them, the ultra-lightweight twins scooped the manufacturer's award.

In honour of the event Triumph launched a very special model – the TR5 Trophy. A versatile, dual-purpose machine, this used a single carburettor in place of the roadster's twin-carb setup, and the engine was much more softly tuned. But in its heyday club riders could use it as everyday transport, and at the weekend remove the headlamp in minutes and be competitive in any form of off-road competition.

No larger than a contemporary off-road single but with a much brisker performance, Triumph's handsome Trophy model was an instant hit.

Triumph GP/TR5 (1948-51)

Years in production: 1948-50 (GP), 1948-58 (TR5)

Engine type: 180 degree parallel twin ohv four-stroke

Bore and stroke: 63 x 80mm

Capacity: 498cc

Compression ratio: 6:1 (TR5)

Power: 40 bhp (GP), 25bhp (TR5) @ 6000rpm

Carburettors: Amal Mk 6

Tyres (front/rear): 3 x 20in/4 x 19in

Wheelbase: 53in

Weight: 295lb (TR5)

Top speed: 85mph (TR5)

Vincent Rapide

Vincent Rapide (1948)

Years in production: 1946-50

Frame: 50 degree V-twin ohv four-stroke

Capacity: 998cc

Bore and stroke: 84 x 90mm

Compression ratio: 6.45:1

Power: 45bhp @ 5300rpm

Carburettors: $1\frac{1}{16}$in Amals

Tyres (front/rear): 3 x 20in/ $3\frac{1}{2}$ x 19in

Wheelbase: $56\frac{1}{2}$in

Top speed: 110mph

Power and speed: it's a formula that sells superbikes today, although in the grim period of postwar austerity few could afford such luxuries. But who could resist the pull of a one litre machine that advertised itself as 'The World's Fastest Standard Motorcycle'? Phil Vincent and his designer Phil Irving had begun to plan the successor to their Series A Rapide as early as 1943, working on their ideas after hours, or when the Stevenage factory's war work schedule permitted. The machine was to be a 1000cc high-speed, ultra-reliable touring bike.

The layout of the engine was similar to that of the 'Plumber's Nightmare' Series A, but cleaned up with unit construction and smooth alloy castings. Even so, the power unit was still slightly longer than before. To make the bike itself more compact, Irving and Vincent came up with a radical solution. The engine and gearbox unit was so massive and rugged that they could do away with the frame. This had the double advantage that there was no need for the conventional frame tubing that was then in short supply. Instead of a frame, the rear swinging arm pivoted directly behind the gearbox, while on top of the engine a sheet steel box was bolted, which formed an attachment for the rear suspension and the steering head for the front forks. Cleverly, it also doubled as the oil tank.

The forks were conventional Brampton girders, which would later be replaced with Vincent's own design. The twin drum brakes of the Series A remained – at first with steel drums, later with alloy. Convenience was also a feature of the design, which abounded with practical features for the rider. Footrests and pedals were adjustable to suit the length of riders' legs and even the size of their feet. Among other firsts was a dual seat with a linkage that allowed it to move independently of the suspension. The kickstart could be fitted to either side of the bike, which allowed it to be used with a sidecar on the right or the left. Click-stop adjusters made light work of common chores such as chain

tensioning, and tommy bars were fitted to the wheels so they could be removed with a minimum of tools.

When the new Rapide was launched in 1946 it caused a sensation – but by law, at least 75 per cent had to go for export, making the machine a rare beast in the early years. In any case, its price made it a luxury item, and since the factory recommended a thorough warm-up for the engine, with a trip of at least 12 miles, it would have been a poor choice for riding to work - but who would want to?

Vincent claimed 45bhp for the engine – low by modern standards, but astounding for its day and the poor quality 'pool' petrol of the time. And it was good enough for 110mph, a staggering speed for those days.

Two years later, Vincent topped even this, launching the legendary Black Shadow. With a massive 5in, 150mph speedometer, it was obvious that this was meant for speed. And it delivered it, with 10hp more than the Rapide and 125mph performance, straight from the crate. Excellent brakes, roadholding and steering made it one of the world's most desirable motorcycles, particularly after Rollie Free took one to a world record of over 150mph at Bonneville Salt Flats in 1948.

A legend was born.

As befitted the 'world's fastest' standard motorcycle, the Rapide is an imposing machine, dominated by the castings of its engine. In contrast, the Brampton forks fitted to the series B give a rather spindly look to the front end; they were soon replaced by Vincent's own Girdraulics.

Velocette KTT

Velocette's enormously successful KTT series had been steadily developed for 14 years when the MkVIII appeared at the Earls Court Show in 1938. Priced at £120, the model was another 'race replica' in the great Velocette tradition, and included a host of innovations seen on the works machines that had won that year's Junior TT.

With a host of lightweight alloy parts, sophisticated oiling and a pioneering rear suspension design, it showed all the benefits of a consistent programme of race development. The most noticeable feature of the engine was its massive cylinder head casting, with its squared-off light alloy fins virtually filling the frame. This had been introduced on the works racers in 1937 and

sold to the public as a limited run of Mk VII KTTs early in 1938. Similar finning extended to the rocker box, which contained a labyrinth of oilways to lubricate the bevel gears and cams.

The Mk VII had a fairly modest state of tune (with an 8.75:1 compression ratio) and a rigid frame with few special fittings. The Mk VIII was an altogether different proposition. It featured 'swinging arm' rear suspension and Dowty oleo pneumatic rear shock absorbers, in which the springing was by air under pressure, with oil damping. It had lightweight magnesium alloy brake hubs and a telescopic housing for

Velocette Mk VIII KTT (1949)

Years in production: 1938-50

Engine type: single-cylinder overhead-
cam four stroke

Bore and stroke: 74 x 81mm

Capacity: 348cc

Compression ratio: 10.9:1

Top speed: 110mph

the front fork spring, while the engine had been beefed up to an 11:1 compression ratio. The valves on the works bikes were filled with sodium for better cooling.

Ridden by Stanley Woods, the Mk VIII won the 1939 Junior TT for the second year running, just after Velocette's great designer Harold Willis had died of meningitis. The model did well in private hands too – one privately owned KTT became the only 350 to lap the Brooklands circuit at more than 100mph on petrol rather than alcohol racing fuel.

War then brought a close to racing as to so many other things, and Velocette built around 2200 versions of its pushrod models for military use. When production resumed after the war the Mk VIII was good enough to take two 350cc world championships and to win the Junior TT three years running.

The postwar engines used the lower compression ratio head, owing to the restriction of fuel to low-octane 'pool' petrol. Production continued until 1950, by which time the double overhead-cam Manx Nortons were taking the honours in world class 350cc racing. But with a top speed of 105mph, the production models enjoyed a long competitive career in the hands of enthusiastic amateurs, who continued to celebrate the brilliance of a design that enjoyed almost a quarter of a century at the top.

Velocette's pivoted fork rear suspension design was innovative at a time when most manufacturers were toying with plungers, if they had embraced rear springing at all. On this example, the early air-sprung rear dampers have been replaced by a later type.

LE Velocette

One of a number of postwar designs aimed at producing everyday transport for everyman, the LE Velocette owed little to convention and featured many interesting concepts. But although it enjoyed a production run of some 16 years, like all its peers that dared to be different, the little Velocette was ultimately unsuccessful, never meeting its maker's optimistic sales target.

In the early postwar years, the bulk of Velocette's production consisted of updated versions of their prewar pushrod models, the MSS and MOV. But in 1948 the firm unveiled the new design that would take their place. Literally, indeed, for the model that Velocette were introducing was designed for mass production, and building it needed all the space the factory could provide.

Its design owed little to anything that had been seen before. The 'frame' was a pressed-steel box, which offered the same advantages that had been seen in the car industry, of quick, cheap and strong

construction – albeit with the disadvantages that it was costly to tool up and difficult to change the design.

The telescopic forks were bang up-to-the-minute, while the rear swinging-arm suspension was state-of-the art, with shock absorber units that could be moved in curved upper mounting slots to change the spring rate and damping – a Velocette patent.

Cleanliness, quietness and convenience were important features of the design, which was intended to appeal to people who would not consider a conventional motorcycle. Voluminous mudguards, built-in legshields and footboards looked after the cleanliness, while convenience included built-in luggage capacity, a hand starter lever (matched by a hand gearchange on the early models), and shaft drive housed in one leg of the swinging arm.

It was the quiet aspect that dictated the choice of the engine design. A horizontally-opposed twin, the design offered smoothness and a low centre of gravity, in addition to an easy transmission run to the shaft drive. The side-valve design allowed the engine to be relatively narrow, while watercooling helped to keep the noise levels low, at the same time allowing the engine to be tucked away while keeping the temperature under control.

The model name LE was chosen for 'little engine', and little it was. Just 149cc when it first appeared, the Velocette fitted most of its designers' objectives, but although the engine was easy to start, its performance was decidedly limited.

Other weaknesses and teething troubles came to light, mainly to do with the lubrication system and transmission – and in 1950 the LE was redesigned. It now had a 192cc engine, with internal modifications, developing some 8bhp.

Sales were slow, for although the potential for a utility bike is enormous (as the later scooters and even more successful Honda step-thrus were to

LE Velocette (1950)

Years in production: 1948-68 (variants including Valiant and Vogue)

Engine type: horizontally-opposed side-valve four-stroke twin

Bore and stroke: 50 x 49mm

Capacity: 192cc

Power: 8 bhp @ 5000 rpm

Top speed: 52mph

prove), this is probably the hardest market of all to crack. What kept the LE in production for so long was its appeal to the police, who found it a perfect choice for urban patrol work. This led to the nickname 'Noddy' bike, supposedly as the result of a directive that police patrolmen meeting a superior officer should nod rather than salute, which would have meant taking a hand off the handlebars.

A luxury version with twin headlamps and scooter-like bodywork, called the Vogue, failed to catch on – a fate that also befell the Valiant, introduced in 1956. This featured an air-cooled engine and a four-speed foot-change gearbox with kickstart, as well as a 'motorcycle' tube frame and styling.

The gearbox found its way on to the LE in 1958, the last major change to the design. The LE continued to be sold in small numbers into the 1960s, but long before this, the disappointing level of sales had forced Velocette to return to building conventional motorcycles, a range that would outlast the LE by over a decade, although the last police 'Noddy' bikes remained in service until 1971.

A motorcycle for Everyman, the Velocette LE offered comprehensive weather protection and luggage space, allied to easy starting and a whisper-quiet engine.

BSA Bantam

BSA Bantam (1951)

Years in production: 1948-63

Engine type: piston-ported
two-stroke single

Bore and stroke: 52 x 28mm

Capacity: 123cc

Compressor ratio: 6.5:1

Power: 4.5bhp @ 5000rpm

Top speed: 50mph

One of the most successful lightweights ever produced in Britain, the Bantam was actually 'borrowed' from a prewar German design.

Before World War II the German manufacturer DKW was one of the great innovators of two-stroke technology. Until then most two-strokes had used a cumbersome 'deflector piston' which had a massive hump in the middle to control the flow of gases. DKW's version used a symmetrical, flat-top piston – together with clever transfer porting – to direct the gas flow for better power and reliability.

As part of the reparations of war, German designs were offered to the Allies. One such was the DKW RT125, a popular little prewar lightweight. The design was turned down by Villiers, Britain's major maker of lightweight two-stroke engines, but was rapidly adopted by BSA. The same design was also taken up by the other Allies. Harley-Davidson, Voskhod and WSK all made their own variants – in the latter cases, for decades later. Even Yamaha borrowed the design.

Although the BSA was a direct copy, the original design had the gearchange on the left in European, rather than

British fashion. So BSA simply reversed the drawings to make a mirror image of the DKW with a 'conventional' gearchange. Inside the egg-shaped engine castings was a three-speed gearbox in unit with the engine, which had a pressed-up full-circle flywheel. The cylinder barrel of cast iron contained opposed transfer ports, and the cylinder head was of aluminium alloy; capacity was 123cc. Lubrication was by petroil mix, fed by a tiny $\frac{5}{8}$ in carburettor with integral air filter. Ignition and lighting were by a Wipac flywheel magneto fitted to the left of the crankshaft. Lighting was direct, with no battery fitted.

The new BSA was announced early in 1948, and initially it was suggested that it would be supplied as a proprietary engine unit only. But in June that year the first complete machine was launched. As was common at the time, it was

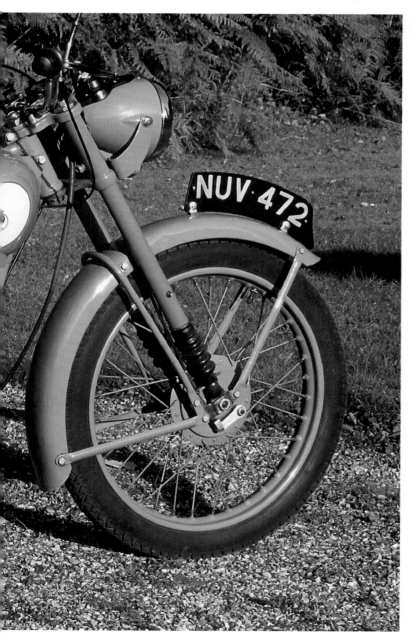

first listed 'for export only' and called the D1. However, by October it had gained the Bantam name, and gradually became available on the home market.

The first model had a rigid frame made of welded steel tubes, a somewhat crude, undamped front fork and front mudguard with a distinct deep valance that was even bigger than the rear. The silencer was teardrop-shaped and very flat in section. Producing $4\frac{1}{2}$ bhp, it was good for about 50mph on a miserly 120mpg, and despite a few niggles, with its £60 price tag, the model sold as fast as BSA could produce it. The finish was mist green, except for pale cream-yellow panels on the sides of the tank.

In 1950 the Bantam was improved and updated with an optional plunger rear suspension, deeper rear mudguard valance and smaller front one, as well as many minor refinements. A new electrical system based on a Lucas alternator was also offered. A competition version designed for trials or scrambles was also catalogued, while some owners modified machines for lightweight racing.

In 1954 a larger 150cc version called the D3 was introduced. It had heavier forks, plunger springing as standard, and a larger front brake, among minor variations. It gained a new swinging-arm frame in 1956, but this was dropped in 1957. The D1 continued in production until August 1963 with little change. There were minor improvements to the electrics, engine and frame, and in 1956 the rigid version was dropped. It had sold some 20,000 a year and was much-loved by owners all around the world. A workhorse whose duties had included telegram deliveries, commuting and farming in the Australian bush, examples soldiered on for a decade or more as a mainstay of some rider training schemes. Meanwhile, derivatives of the original design would continue to be produced as late as 1971.

Plunger rear springing added comfort to the original D I's rigid rear end, but both front and rear suspension remained undamped except by friction.

Norton Model 18 & ES2

Norton Model 18 & ES2 (1947/52)

Years in production: 1921-54 (Model 18),
  1928-63 (ES2)

Engine type: single-cylinder side-valve
  four-stroke

Bore and stroke: 79 x 100mm

Capacity: 490cc

Compression ratio: 6.45:1

Power: 21bhp

Carburettor: Amal Monobloc 276
  (1947 Mod 18)

Ignition: Magneto (prior to 1958)

Weight: 374 lb (1947 Mod 18)

Top speed: 78mph

Pushrod Norton singles date back to 1922, but their heyday really began in 1924 when they carried the factory to a string of race victories. That role was to last a scant three years, supplanted by the more efficient overhead-cam racers. But as roadsters they would continue until 1963, gradually outclassed in the performance stakes, but offering occasional reminders of their sporting heritage.

The Model 18 was the first pushrod Norton, but it adopted a bottom end and 79 x 100mm that went back almost to the dawn of the marque. It was soon followed by a host of variants, including the 600cc Model 19 and sports ES2. The origin of the latter model number is uncertain; one theory is that it stands for 'Enclosed Springs' for on the first Model 18, pushrod and return springs were both exposed.

The ES2 (above) shared its heritage and most of its fittings with the Model 18. On the immediate postwar models, the most obvious difference between the two was the ES2's plunger rear suspension – a mixed blessing.

Postwar the Model 18 was the first pushrod Norton to go back into production, appearing in 1946 in something similar to its prewar form. In 1947 it gained Norton's famous 'Roadholder' front forks, yet retained a rigid rear end. The ES2, relaunched that year, had Norton's plunger rear suspension – something of a mixed blessing, for although it offered a degree of comfort it also added weight and was a constant maintenance chore.

While Norton advertised on the basis of the company's racing heritage, in truth they were simply good, solid sporting singles, robust and torquey; the handling, roadholding and brakes were predictable and sure. Many were used as sidecar tugs, still more, simply as basic transport. The Model 18 was also sold for trials use, but from 1949 to 1954 Norton offered a proper trials variant, the rigid 500T with a frame based on the wartime 16H. The trials models relied on the upright Norton gearbox originally fitted to the Model 18, but from 1950 on the roadsters gained the so-called laid-down gearbox, which offered a neater enclosure for the change mechanism.

A slow process of development followed and in 1953 the ES2 gained the swinging-arm frame used on the first Dominator twins. In 1954 the rigid Model 18 was phased out and the 600cc Model 19 was reintroduced in rigid (mainly for sidecar use) or swinging-arm frame. A 350cc the Model 50, joined the range in 1956, and a new gearbox with a triangular selection mechanism was fitted to all the singles.

In 1959 the Model 19 disappeared and the smaller variants found a new home – the revered Featherbed frame. After 1961 the singles gained the new Slimline frame, and this was the final chapter in their story. From then on, Norton would concentrate of their twins range, while the 1965/66 ES2 Mk2 was nothing more than a cynically rebadged Matchless.

Norton's 'long Roadholder' forks were fitted to the Model 18 from 1947. They offered good handling at the expense of a slightly heavy appearance at the front end.

BSA A10 Golden Flash

BSA's postwar parallel twins owed an obvious debt to Triumph's trend-setting Speed Twin of the 1930s, but in every detail the design was a true original. And in its own way, BSA was as influential as Triumph in making the layout such a staple of the British industry in the 1950s and into the 1960s.

There was a further link with Triumph, since some of the earliest design work on what would become BSA's twin was carried out by Val Page, the engineer responsible for the first

Solid, dependable and economical, the 650cc A10 twin shared a common heritage with Triumph's Speed Twin but had a character that was all its own.

Triumph parallel twin, the 650cc 6/1. Yet more design studies were carried out by Edward Turner, designer of the Speed Twin, during some time spent at BSA in the war years. Most of the detail work, however, was the responsibility of BSA chief designer Herbert Perkins, who had been with the company for many years. He was nearing retirement age when he laid down the basis of the 500cc BSA A7, which was launched in 1946.

Among notable differences from the Triumph design were the use of a single camshaft with four lobes, carried behind the engine, instead of separate ones for exhaust and inlet. The gearbox was also bolted to the back of the engine in semi-unit construction, instead of being completely

Plunger rear springing (above), a contemporary fad, offered only limited movement in comparison with rigid frames. Uneven chain tension could result in rapid chain wear, while wear in the under-lubricated suspension system itself would result in vague handling.

offered with the then-new plunger suspension system, which supposedly added to rider comfort, although as time would tell, at the expense of handling as the plungers wore. A rigid version was available until 1952, mainly for the benefit of sidecar users, for whom there was also alternative gearing. Perhaps the only serious weakness – especially for sidecar use – was the poor braking from the narrow steel drums originally fitted.

As the years wore on, there was a steady stream of improvements and options for both the A7 and A10. These included sports versions with high-performance carburettors and tuned engines. The first major change came in 1954, with the adoption of a new frame and swinging-arm rear suspension. This necessitated a change to the transmission. Alloy brake drums followed in 1956, with a corresponding improvement in stopping power. This was needed even more by the sports-tuned Road Rocket, introduced that year and good for 110mph.

The Golden Flash itself went on year by year, earning a reputation for dependability that endeared it to a generation of riders. As fashions changed, so BSA developed the unit-engined A65 model, and the A10 was phased out in 1961, although the more sporting Super Rocket continued until 1963. That last year saw the introduction of the definitive sporting derivative, the Rocket Gold Star. This used a tuned 650cc sports engine in a Gold Star frame – a hybrid that worked so well that it overshadowed BSA's own replacement for the pre-unit 650cc twins. It was a fitting swan song for a much loved model.

A handsome engine (below), proudly bearing BSA's 'piled arms' badge on the timing cover, the iron-barrelled A10 power unit had many detail differences compared to the rival Triumph and Norton offerings.

separate. The power from the earliest engines was 26bhp and the power unit was mounted in a duplex cradle frame with rigid rear end and telescopic forks that gave competent handling. A sports version was offered two years later. Some problems with the transmission and other features such as the lubrication were tackled in the ensuing years to make the A7 into a competent and reliable mount, though not one with a particularly high performance.

Much of the work involved in refining the original design was carried out by Bert Hopwood, a very experienced designer who had worked at most of the major factories. He soon had a further brief, for when news of Triumph's plans to introduce a larger version of their twin leaked out, BSA decided to follow suit, with a deadline of October 1949, the Earls Court Show. Starting in May 1949, the design work was carried out in around four weeks, and the model was in prototype form inside five months. Short-cuts had to be taken – such as ordering the tooling and assuming that there would be no major design changes – and many of the parts were shared with the 500cc A7. Even so, it was an incredible effort, with prototypes being continuously tested by teams of riders from the month of August onwards.

The rush job proved to be worth it, as the A10 Golden Flash was a success from the start, with few problems to mar its path to public acceptance. The Golden Flash name referred to the paint scheme, applied overall, although black and chrome was offered as an option. The new iron-barrelled engine gave a useful 35bhp and the machine was

BSA A10 Golden Flash (1952)

Years in production: 1950-61

Engine type: twin-cylinder overhead-valve four-stroke

Bore and stroke: 70 x 84mm

Capacity: 646cc

Compression ratio: 6.5:1

Power: 35bhp at 4500rpm

Gearbox: four-speed

Weight: 395lb (plunger)

Royal Enfield Bullet

Royal Enfield's much loved range of Bullet singles typify much of the best of British tradition. Unglamorous, but sturdy and reliable workhorses, they also possess the virtually unique distinction of having remained in volume production for a period approaching half a century.

The Bullet name, which harked back to Royal Enfield's association with gun manufacture, first appeared in the early 1930s. It was applied to a full range of 250, 350 and 500cc overhead-valve singles – lighter, tuned sports versions of the firm's existing models. But it was with the 350cc model that the name was most associated from the outset, and the Bullet range was particularly aimed at the sport of trials, which in those days was contested by modified road machines with little more special equipment than a high-level silencer.

With the start of the war Royal Enfield became a major supplier of motorcycles to the armed forces, some 30,000 of them being the overhead-valve 350cc WD/CO, based heavily on the prewar trials machines. These formed the backbone of the first few years of the

company's peacetime production, but in February 1948 the first postwar Bullet appeared.

Appropriately enough, the prototypes were entered in an important trial, where two first-class awards were gained. The Bullet was a pioneer of swinging-arm suspension, using two oil-damped shock absorber units carried at a steep angle on a pair of lugs that extended up from the frame. Although rear suspension was starting to gain favour for road use, it was much derided for trials, where the emphasis had always been on keeping the rear wheel in contact with the ground and relying on a slogging motor to carry the machine through.

It was later on in 1948 that the Bullet really started to prove itself by winning the trophy at the International Six Days' Trial, the ISDT, where two riders also took gold medals, the only ones awarded to 350s.

Royal Enfield Bullet (1952)

Years in production: 1948-1996

Engine type: single-cylinder ohv four-stroke

Bore and stroke: 70 x 90mm

Capacity: 346cc

Compression ratio: 6.2:1

Power: 18bhp

Gearbox: Albion

Carburettors: 1 in Amal

Tyres: $3\frac{1}{4}$ x 19in

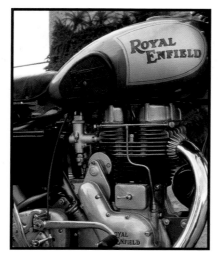

The unmistakable shape of the Bullet engine (left) is visible in machines made four decades later in India, although more modern electrics have replaced the Magdyno behind the cylinder.

The production models came onto the market the next year, and were broadly similar to the prototypes. Following a Royal Enfield convention, the engine appeared to be a wet-sump design, but actually used an oil tank cast as part of the crankcase. The gearbox, a four-speed Albion design, was bolted to the back of this, resulting in a compact and rigid unit as befitted its competition status. The new frame had a single front downtube and swinging-arm rear suspension, as well as Enfield's own telescopic forks at the front. Both wheels had 6in brakes, and the rear wheel incorporated Enfield's cush-drive hub.

The new design was such a success that the competition version was soon joined by road bikes, while the trials and scrambles machines continued winning. In 1952, Johnny Brittain won the Scottish Six Days' Trial, and the following year he and fellow Enfield rider Jack Stocker were part of the team that won the ISDT without losing a single point.

The Bullets were developed over the ensuing years. A 500cc version appeared in 1953 – alloy brakes were introduced, and a new styling feature, the cast-alloy Casquette, formed a combined steering head, instrument panel and light housing. A revised frame was introduced in 1956, while Enfield's own full-enclosure fairing, the Airflow, was optional. A works replica trials version was catalogued in 1958, and there were a number of other variants before the Bullet range was dropped in 1962. But not quite. While Royal Enfield themselves used the name on a number of later models, the rights to manufacture the original had been sold to a company in Madras, India. Slowly developed over the decades, it remains in production in a variety of versions – eloquent testament to the soundness of the basic design.

With its upswept silencer and swinging-arm frame, the compact Bullet hints at its original trials derivation.

Sunbeam S8

The Sunbeam carried its ammeter and switch (left) on the battery box above the gear box and behind the engine where they were invisible to the rider.

Designed as Britain's answer to the BMW, the Sunbeam S7 and later the S8 were an odd mixture of the inspired and the impractical, which ultimately condemned them to being an interesting backwater, rather than part of the mainstream of postwar motorcycling.

Several influences were at work, but the new machines were BSAs in all but name. Sunbeam had ceased to be a truly separate entity during the 1930s, and the trademarks now belonged to the giant BSA organisation, which reasoned that they could capitalise on Sunbeam's 'gentleman's motorcycle' image for their new tourer.

The design was the work of independent designer Erling Poppe, but was heavily based on the BMW R75, manufacturing rights to which had been offered to BSA as part of the war reparations. But while the double-cradle frame and telescopic fork echoed the BMW, the engine unit was a completely new design.

Displacing 487cc, the engine was basically a parallel twin not unlike that offered by BSA themselves in the form of the A7. But it was housed in alloy castings and turned around so that the crankshaft ran in line with the frame. And it seemed like a more sophisticated design than most contemporary motorcycles, thanks to the use of an overhead-cam, driven by a cam-chain at the front of the crankcase.

Sunbeam S8 (1952)

Years in production: 1946-56

Engine type: parallel twin (in-line) overhead-cam four-stroke

Bore and stroke: 70 x 63.5mm

Capacity: 487cc

Power: 24 bhp @ 6000rpm

Carburettor: Amal

Tyres (front/rear): 4¾ x 16in/ 4¾ x 16in

Wheelbase: 57in

Weight: 430lb (S7) 413lb (S8)

The first of the Sunbeam's problems arose from the choice of transmission. The intention was to use a shaft drive like the BMW, but for some reason the design adopted had a worm gear in place of the German machine's bevels. While much easier to manufacture, it was inherently weak, and on prototypes the worm was shown to strip its thread if the engine was used to its full potential. Rather than redesign the drive, BSA chose to cut the power – emasculating the engine to a paltry 24 bhp unit that the worm could handle. The second problem was vibration. This had been evident on the prototypes, but the warning signs were

ignored until the bike went into production in 1946. When an initial batch was despatched to a police team intended to escort George VI on an official visit, it was reported that they were unridable. This time, the 'solution' was to replace the rigid engine mountings with flexible rubber buffers, allowing the engine to shake without communicating this to the rider. A consequence of this action was that a rust-prone section of flexible pipe had to be added in front of the silencer, which did not move with the engine.

The machine weighed more than 400lb – but looked heavier. Fitted with 16in 'balloon' tyres, its handling was prone to vagueness, which became aggravated as the plunger rear suspension units wore. Nor was it much success as a sidecar puller – the result of its limited power ouput. The finish, in BSA's rather drab 'Mist Green', can hardly have helped its showroom appeal, any more than the stories of its mechanical defects, and it was a poor seller.

In 1949 BSA decided to tackle both the performance and the styling by launching the new S8 as a sports alternative to the touring S7. Much lighter than its predecessor, this used cycle parts such as forks and wheels from other BSA models. It was a more popular machine than the S7, but was still far from a runaway success. BSA finally discontinued the Sunbeams in 1956.

Handsome and more conventional, the S8 answered many of the problems of the original S7, but it still suffered from the same mechanical weaknesses.

Vincent Black Prince

Phil Vincent was nothing if not a great innovator. Having pioneered his own suspension design and created the fastest road vehicle of its time, in 1954 riders expected Vincent's latest Series D to be something special. Indeed it was, for here was Vincent describing the lack of weather protection as a Stone Age idea and offering a pioneering, fully enclosed aerodynamic motorcycle.

As events would prove, this was a serious miscalculation on his part, for the customers who had loved the brutal exposed engines of his earlier machines were left cold by the Series D styling. Technically it was superb, and offered a glimpse of the fully faired sports machines of the future. Press tests extolled its weather protection, economy and speed, but all-important sales were slow to follow. Meanwhile, the competition was becoming faster, better suspended and, above all, cheap.

Yet Vincent's logic was impeccable. All motorcycles were facing competition from lower-priced cars, at a time when both still represented alternative modes of transport rather than leisure accessories. The Vincent was already faster and handled better than almost any motorcycle – so convenience must have seemed a logical route for improvement. And Phil Vincent had even consulted the owner's club about suggested innovations.

The Series D modifications were applied to the whole range: the Rapide, Black Shadow, Black Knight and range-leading Black Prince. Under the skin, technical changes included coil ignition and several engineering alterations. The chassis underwent major modification, for the fabricated steel backbone that formed an oil tank was replaced by a simple tube, which proved much weaker, and separate tank. There was a new rear subframe/seat support and an old Rudge idea was recycled, for there was a hand lever to remove the chore of putting the bike on its stand.

Problems with supply of the glass-fibre components meant that some Series D machines were supplied in naked form. Even so, being designed to be hidden, many thought the appearance ugly.

Motorcycle sales were slow – too slow to provide the much needed cash. Meanwhile another Vincent venture would help to deal a death blow to the company. Just as the Series D anticipated the fully faired sports tourer, the Amanda water scooter predated the jet ski by a quarter of a century. But technical and safety problems, plus the discovery that Vincent was actually losing money on bike sales, pushed the company into closure. The last Vincent was built barely a week before Christmas 1955. It is a strange twist of fate that the enclosed models, through rarity, are now among the most sought-after of the survivors.

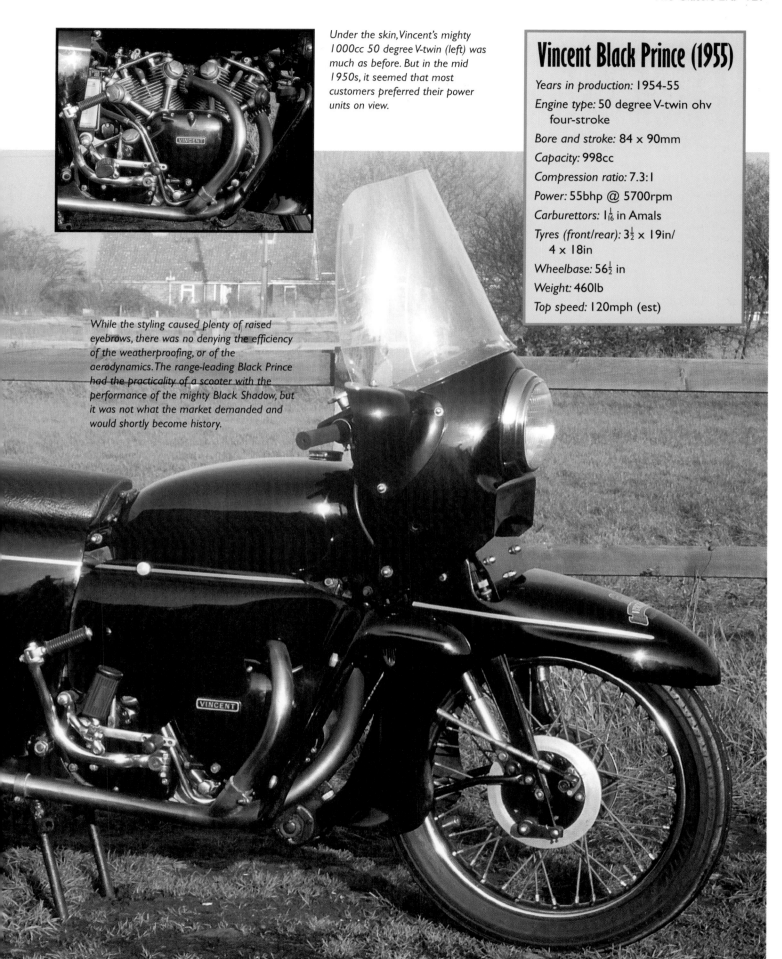

Under the skin, Vincent's mighty 1000cc 50 degree V-twin (left) was much as before. But in the mid 1950s, it seemed that most customers preferred their power units on view.

Vincent Black Prince (1955)

Years in production: 1954-55

Engine type: 50 degree V-twin ohv four-stroke

Bore and stroke: 84 x 90mm

Capacity: 998cc

Compression ratio: 7.3:1

Power: 55bhp @ 5700rpm

Carburettors: $1\frac{1}{16}$ in Amals

Tyres (front/rear): $3\frac{1}{2}$ x 19in/ 4 x 18in

Wheelbase: $56\frac{1}{2}$ in

Weight: 460lb

Top speed: 120mph (est)

While the styling caused plenty of raised eyebrows, there was no denying the efficiency of the weatherproofing, or of the aerodynamics. The range-leading Black Prince had the practicality of a scooter with the performance of the mighty Black Shadow, but it was not what the market demanded and would shortly become history.

Ariel Square Four

Ariel's Square Four always had a special place in motorcycling mythology, almost regardless of how well it performed. A four-cylinder machine when such a thing was almost impossibly exotic, it was also a 1000cc machine at a time when a 650 or even a 500 was considered a big bike.

And from 1955, when Vincent ceased manufacture, the Square Four was by far the largest capacity machine on offer from the British industry.

The Square Four was an idea long before it was a workable bike. The idea started back in 1928, when Edward

A handsome machine, the late 1000cc version of Ariel's long-lived range leader was positioned as luxury tourer rather than sports bike. Tank-top flutes were a traditional Ariel styling feature, although by 1956 the company was but a part of the giant BSA group.

Turner – later to become famous as the designer of the Triumph twin and the head of the Triumph company – was a young hopeful hawking sketches of a revolutionary machine around the motorcycle industry.

The idea found a home at Ariel, then one of Britain's most important manufacturers, who took it up enthusiastically. What Turner had sketched was effectively a pair of across-the-frame parallel twins linked by a pair of gears. While there were theoretical problems

Four pipes typify the MkII postwar machine (right), while the large oil tank wrapping around the engine was first introduced in 1956.

with the linking gears, the beauty of the scheme was its incredible compactness and the fact that all the opposing forces could be balanced to result in a super-smooth engine.

The original prototype was a 500, so small and light that it could be fitted into the frame of the contemporary Ariel 250. Easy to start and smooth, it used an overhead-camshaft that probably contributed to its major weakness – overheating around the cylinder head. But after considerable development a revised version that was unveiled in autumn 1930 created a sensation. The machine had an obvious appeal for sidecar riders and in 1932 was offered in a 600cc form better suited to this use, while the 500 was dropped.

That the Square Four had speed potential was obvious, and so it was proved in 1933 when Ben Bickell took a much-modified 500 (a small-bore 600 fitted with a supercharger) to Brooklands. The machine narrowly failed to become the first British 500 to achieve 100 miles in an hour, despite lapping at well over 110. Every attempt failed as a result of the overheating bugbear.

In 1937 the engine was completely redesigned, partly to get around such problems. The overhead-cam was abandoned in favour of pushrods, and the crankcase and crank were completely altered. For the first time, a 1000cc version joined the 600, and as an option, rear springing using the link system devised by Frank Anstey was offered. This gave constant chain tension but little movement, and required frequent attention to its numerous plain bushes to prevent slop setting in.

After the war only the larger version went back into production, now with a modern telescopic fork. It was heavier than it should have been, however, and in 1949 the engine became all-alloy, gaining coil ignition with a car-type distributor a year later. Acceleration and handling both improved, while the cooling also got better.

The final development came in 1953 when the MkII version appeared. Sporting four separate exhaust pipes and numerous internal improvements, this was a flexible machine that proved an excellent high-speed tourer.

That was to be virtually the end, however. The 'Squariel' was growing ever more expensive against the competition and the minor refinements introduced each year could not mask the fact that in some areas, such as cooling and rear suspension, it was not as refined as it could be. The year 1958 was the last year of full production, although the concept was developed as late as the 1970s by the Healey brothers, who put a modified Square Four engine in a frame built by the Swiss specialist Egli to complete around 20 specials – while Turner's linked crankshaft idea was employed to great effect by Kawasaki and others in racing.

Ariel Square Four (1956)

Years in production: 1953-58 (4G Mk II)

Engine type: four-cylinder (square four) ohv four-stroke

Bore and stroke: 65 x 75mm

Capacity: 997cc

Compression ratio: 6.45:1

Power: 42bhp @ 5800rpm

Carburettor: SU

Weight: 460lb

Top speed: 107mph

Douglas Dragonfly

Against a background of financial uncertainty, the Douglas factory was always willing to rise to the challenge, pioneering innovative designs and modern styling. And so it was in 1954, when they launched a sophisticated and original looking design at the Earls Court show.

Developed during 1953, the model was intended to supersede the rather dated range then in production and take the company into a new era. Many of its design features foreshadowed those of the slightly later BMW, which went on to achieve considerable success.

Douglas' new engine design was a 350 based on their previous engine – which had enjoyed only slow sales despite a good performance – although it also borrowed heavily from an interesting 500cc prototype shown in 1951. The engine had been strengthened internally and cleaned up externally, with a streamlined appearance and a

crankcase that housed the electrics and other ancillaries, while the gearbox was attached to the rear. A single Amal Monobloc carburettor fed both cylinders. Coil ignition and alternator electrics were among the model's advanced features.

Most of the cycle parts were bought in – a departure from Douglas' normal practice. The frame was completely new, being an open duplex construction of welded tubes, manufactured on their behalf by the Reynolds Tube Company. A swinging arm with twin dampers (a modern feature for the time) looked after the rear suspension, while the front suspension used a design patented by

A handsome machine with the styling of a miniature BMW, the Dragonfly's obvious charms were let down by a lack of power and the company's limited finances, which prevented it being fully developed.

Douglas Dragonfly (1956)

Years in production: 1953-56

Engine type: horizontally-opposed
   twin-cylinder four-stroke

Bore and stroke: 60.8 x 60mm

Capacity: 348cc

Ignition: Coil, with Miller alternator

Carburettor: Amal Monobloc

Weight: 365lb

Top speed: 75mph

Midlands engineer Ernie Earles and built by Reynolds. This used a long swinging arm, controlled by twin dampers. A similar design was used by BMW on their production bikes, while MV Agusta, among others, tried it for racing.

The other main styling feature was the petrol tank and light unit. Containing a massive $5\frac{1}{2}$ gallons, the tank pressing continued forward of the steering head to house the headlamp and instrument panel, which did not turn with the steering.

Originally called the 'Dart', by the time of the show the model was called the 'Dragonfly'. Finished in a cream shade called 'light stone' with toning green panels or black-and-gold, it was an attractive if unconventional machine.

Unfortunately, after its much-vaunted show launch – when it appeared clamped between the jaws of a giant micrometer – Douglas was unable to offer quantity production for another nine months. Despite a favourable road test in April 1955, the price had gone up by almost 10 per cent by August, and a less favourable road test appeared in September.

Its handling could not be faulted, although the brakes were rather poor. But ultimately the problem for the Dragonfly came down to a mismatch of its capacity and its presentation. With the styling and fittings of a long-distance tourer, it had an engine that was pushed to top 75mph and cruised at considerably less.

It found few customers – only around 1500 were made – and Douglas' shaky finances did not help. Towards the end of 1956 the company was taken over by the Westinghouse electrical group, and production of motorcycles ended the following March.

Norton Dominator

Inspired by the popular success of Triumph's prewar Speed Twin, and aware that other factories were working on their own versions, Norton realised that if they were to have any future after World War II, they too needed a twin engine.

The job was undertaken by Bert Hopwood, who had worked on the development of Edward Turner's original Speed Twin design and had a vast experience in the industry. In 1947 Hopwood laid out his design, which aimed to improve on the Triumph's weaknesses, such as poor cooling, and incorporated some new ideas of his own. Chief among these was the use of only a single camshaft for inlet and exhaust valves, in place of the two used by Triumph and all the other factories.

The design had to work within the constraints of Norton's antiquated manufacturing machinery, as well as running on the poor quality postwar 'Pool' petrol. And for reasons of economy, it had to fit into the existing single-cylinder model's frame. Such thoughts as these were behind the choice of a single carburettor, with close inlet ports and splayed exhausts.

Fitted into plunger cycle parts from the range-leading ES2 single, with some cosmetic changes including a special tank and mudguards, this became the Norton Model 7 Dominator, launched in 1949. However it was the middle of the year before any Dominators found their way on to the home market.

With a soft tuning, it offered little real challenge to Triumph's twin – being more expensive to the tune of some £20 – and was little promoted by Norton against their traditional singles for the first few years. But it would still reach 90mph and offered excellent reliability and handling in the Norton tradition.

Flat Norton handlebars contributed to a comfortable riding position (right) and the famous 'Roadholder' forks assisted in the secure handling.

There was little change during the next few years. In 1953 it gained a swinging-arm rear suspension, and a year later an alloy cylinder head. It was phased out in 1956, having long been overshadowed by its replacement, the De-Luxe, or Dominator 88, which found its way on to the home market in 1953. The engine was much as before, but what made the 88 special was its frame, a close copy of the phenomenally successful 'Featherbed' used on the works Manx Norton racers. With the Featherbed's legendary handling, and weighing some 40lb less than the Model 7, it handled and went rather better than its predecessor. In 1956 the 88 Dominator's engine received the benefit of some serious performance development. The engine was resized by enlarging both bore and stroke to give a new capacity of 600cc. Its power output went up from 29 to 31 bhp and the new model was called the Dominator 99. With a hotter camshaft and higher compression ratio, plus new carburettor, the model's number roughly equated to its top speed. There were refinements to the frame to match the performance, as well as other refinements.

The new engine also went into the Model 7's frame, the resulting machine being aimed at sidecar users.

The next important change was in 1961-62, when a new 49 bhp 650cc model was announced and both the 88 and 99 came out in SS (Super Sports) versions. The 600s were soon discontinued and in 1964 the first of a series of 750 models, the Atlas, appeared.

Norton Dominator (1956)

Years in production: 1956-62 (Dominator 99)

Frame: parallel twin ohv four-stroke

Capacity: 596cc

Bore and stroke: 68 x 82mm

Compression ratio: 7.4:1

Power: 31bhp @ 6500rpm

Carburettors: $1\frac{1}{16}$in Amal 376

Ignition: coil

Wheelbase: $56\frac{1}{2}$in

Weight: 395lb

Top speed: 101mph

With a 'slimline' version of Norton's famous Featherbed frame adding comfort, Norton's Dominator twin offered the best handling package standard package available.

Velocette MSS

Velocette MSS (1956)

Years in production: 1954-68

Engine type: ohv four-stroke single

Bore and stroke: 86 x 86 mm

Capacity: 499 cc

Compression ratio: 6.75:1

Power: 23 bhp @ 5000 rpm

Weight: 375 lb

Top speed: 80 mph

The MSS first appeared in 1935 – a 500cc sports model designed to fit into the 'M' series that comprised the 250 MOV and 350 MAC. Like the rest of the series it was an overhead-valve single with Velocette's own development of a high camshaft driven by intermediate gears, and short pushrods. These were designed to give the low reciprocating masses of an overhead-cam model and similar revvability, and succeeded – giving the MSS a speed not too far short of the company's race-derived 'K' models.

Velocette MACs were among a number of machines produced for military use, but only one MSS was tested by the army, and production ended for the duration. The 'M' series reappeared soon after the war, but as the factory soon put all their efforts into the 'revolutionary' pressed steel LE, all but the MAC (including the old 81 x 96 mm long-stroke 500) were discontinued.

The MAC underwent a steady programme of development throughout the early 1950s. There were many detail changes to the engine, but the most important changes were to the chassis, with Velocette's own telescopic forks appearing in 1951 and a swinging-arm frame using Velocette's patented adjustable shock absorbers in 1953.

The year 1954 saw the relaunch of a model called the MSS, but in truth this was a very different proposition from prewar days. The engine was of much shorter stroke, giving 'square' dimensions in its alloy barrel. The bottom end was similarly updated, and although the engine was softly tuned it was a modern design with considerable in-built strength.

The frame was the same as used on the contemporary MAC, and it was even claimed that the engine dimensions had been dictated by the need to fit it in this chassis. That the model was planned as a tourer was evident from the fitted panniers, which could be supplied as an option, while sidecar lugs were built into the frame. The gearbox was beefed up compared to the earlier MAC's, and sidecar ratios were optional.

Despite the soft tune, the MSS was no slouch, being good for 80 mph or more, while the spring frame offered excellent handling. It was no surprise, therefore, that it started to be tuned for higher performance. In 1955 a very rare scrambles version was offered, while the following year launched the sports Venom model. This began a series in which higher and higher performance was achieved at the expense of the very flexibility and usability that had been the reason for introducing the pushrod models.

The underlying machine changed little, keeping outdated features such as the separate magneto long into the 1960s. It was such factors as the difficulty of obtaining supplies of components, coupled with the factory's increasing financial problems, that contributed to the end of the model in 1968. But its appeal lives on, with the qualities of the long-legged, economical single cylinder engine at the heart of the experience.

Classic single: a prewar finish and prewar virtues were evident in a machine that was relaunched, albeit heavily redesigned, almost 20 years after it first appeared in the 1930s. The major changes centred on the chassis, with modern telescopic forks and swinging-arm suspension, while the engine had been redesigned to give a much shorter stroke.

Norton International

In prewar days, the Norton Model 30 had been the racing flagship of the range, but by World War II the pure racers had already begun to diverge from the International that was on sale to the public. When postwar production resumed in 1947, the 'Inter' had found a niche as a fast sporting roadster, and its single overhead-cam engine had become a vastly different proposition from the double overhead-cam racing Manx models.

The Inters achieved steady, though limited, sales for the next few years, and while some diehard enthusiasts continued to race them in amateur competition, they were becoming dated against competition that included Triumph twins and the BSA Gold Star. Even so, several Clubman's TT winners of the late 1940s were mounted on Internationals fitted with special racing equipment, including an alloy cylinder barrel in place of the roadster's cast iron.

The final stage of development of the Inter came in 1953, when the alloy engine was installed in Norton's latest racing frame, the Featherbed, together with a new gearbox of the current design. In this form the International won its final Clubman's TT, although the Featherbed model was really intended as a sports special for fast road work.

The International's Featherbed frame was not quite a replica of the one used on the pure racers, but it was built to a higher standard than its humbler roadster brothers. In any form, the Featherbed became the standard by which all handling would be judged for two decades, and with some of the best telescopic forks in the business, and braking to match, it could be pushed to the limits of the considerable performance that the Inter's engine could deliver.

As a racing engine the 490cc overhead-cam unit made few concessions to practicality, although it was supremely rugged and reliable. It could be tricky to set up, with running clearances adjusted by a multiplicity of shims, and an oiling system that relied on several hard-to-reach adjustable jets. The valves remained exposed until the end of production, with the result that incurable oil leaks from the valve gear were a constant fact of life for Inter owners. Roadster silencing tended to stifle the engine's performance, and by the late 1950s it was possible to get the same level of power with much less fuss from later designs such as Norton's own Dominator twin.

But such complaints were to miss the point completely, for the International oozed class, with an image second to none and a performance that was more usable than many of its rivals. Full of sound and fury, it handled and braked superbly, and allowed its lucky owner to believe that he was riding a real racer on the road.

Norton Model 30 (1956)

Engine type: single overhead cam
single-cylinder four-stroke

Bore and stroke: 79 ×100mm

Capacity: 490cc

Compression ratio: 7.23:1

Power: 29.5bhp @ 5500rpm

Carburettors: $1\frac{5}{32}$ in Amal TT

Tyres (front/rear): 3 × 19in/
$3\frac{1}{4}$ × 19in

Wheelbase: 55.5in

Top speed: 97mph

The International was always expensive and sold at a very low level. By 1956 it was being made to special order only, and there were detail changes as parts were used up or new fittings were employed. The last of the line left the works in 1958, when fewer than 20 were made. But to the end, the Inter had a pedigree borrowed from some of the most famous British racers ever made, and a performance that kept riders enthralled for decades.

Sharing something of the lines of the Manx racers, the International used a similar Featherbed frame, but an engine based on the prewar single overhead-cam racing power unit.

Rider's eye view (right): Norton's straight handlebars and fork-top instrument panel were standard for the road-going Featherbed framed models. It was only under the tank that the last Norton 'cammy' single displayed its prewar heritage.

BSA Gold Star

The heart of it all: the all-alloy pushrod engine was developed from BSA's prewar Empire Star, mated to a massive Amal GP carburettor and sports gearbox.

Before the war, the BSA Gold Star had already established itself as a legend. Postwar it would go on to become the definitive sports single – unequalled in production racing and a force to be reckoned with in almost every form of motorcycle competition from trials to scrambling (motocross).

The first postwar Goldie appeared at the 1948 Earls Court Show, but had already been seen in competition in amateur racing, including the 1947 Manx Grand Prix and 1948 Clubmans TT. Initially only on sale as a 350cc machine, its design included an alloy head and barrel that enclosed the pushrod tube, and many tuning parts were available from the outset. Most of the cycle parts were based on the contemporary touring B31, though new telescopic forks and a plunger rear suspension were added. A rigid version was on offer for the trials rider.

The top speed of the standard machine was much better than the B31, but on the low-octane fuel available was limited to less than 80mph. Fitted with the factory tuning parts, however, it could top 90mph, with a lively performance throughout the range. In 1949 a Clubmans model so equipped won the amateur 350cc race in the Isle of Man.

A 500cc version went on sale the next year, 1950. Both models gained a larger, 8in front drum brake and were in most respects identical. Detail improvements followed and by 1952 the 350 model could comfortably exceed 95mph. A more obvious change than the engine work, however, was the frame. Of all-welded construction, this had a single top tube and duplex cradle under the engine, kinked on the right-hand side to accommodate the prominent oil pump. Rear suspension was now by an effective swinging-arm design, with the engine and gearbox carried in substantial plates that added to the overall stiffness. By 1954, after steady development, the 350 could top the 'ton' in Clubmans trim. What was to become almost the definitive version of the 500 appeared after 1955 and was given the DB type designation. Fitted with racing accessories, this could top 110mph with ease.

In 1956 the ultimate Goldie appeared. The DBD34 was fitted with a host of race-proven tuning parts. These included what was to become the legendary Gold Star silencer, part racing megaphone, part roadster silencer. On the over-run it produced a characteristic 'twitter' that was to become a well-loved feature. The cylinder head was revised to suit the largest sports carburettor available, the 1½in Amal GP. The gearbox was given ultra-close ratios and needle rollers in the sleeve gear, and its designation RRT2 became part of Gold Star mythology. The front brake was changed to an equally legendary and desirable Goldie component, the 190mm full-width alloy front drum.

In Clubmans trim, the Goldie was fitted with the steeply angled clip-on handlebars, rearset footrests, swept-back exhaust,

Clubmans cockpit (left): steeply angled handlebars, twin clocks, jutting headlamp on tubular brackets – the Goldie look helped to breed a generation of café racers.

BSA Gold Star (1957)

Years in production: 1956-63 (DBD34)

Engine type: single-cylinder ohv four-stroke

Bore and stroke: 85 x 88mm

Capacity: 496cc

Compression ratio: 7.8:1

Power: 40bhp @ 7000rpm (42bhp with megaphone silencer)

Carburettors: $1\frac{1}{2}$in Amal GP

Tyres (front/rear): $2\frac{3}{4}$ x 20in/ $3\frac{1}{2}$ x 19in

Wheelbase: 56in

Weight: 305lb

Top speed: 110mph

The classic 1950s sports single – a BSA Gold Star DBD34 in the Clubmans trim, which included clip-on racing handlebars, rearset footrests, swept-back exhaust and 'twittering' Goldie silencer. Race-tuning extended to the close-ratio gearbox, which enabled a Gold Star to hit 50mph in first gear at the expense of a slow start-off.

light alloy fuel tank and paired speedometer/rev counter that set the style for a generation of 1960s café racers. On the Goldie it was no mere window dressing, for the model so dominated the Isle of Man Clubmans TT that the series became redundant. After its first win in 1949 it won every year until 1956, when the series was discontinued. In that last victorious year, only two of the 350cc field rode anything else. In the 500 race, Gold Stars took all the first six places.

Perhaps the most versatile sports machine of all time, Goldies also won many top-class trials and scrambles, although even during the 1950s it was becoming obvious that the days of heavy off-road singles were numbered. By the end of the decade the works team had switched to works-prepared versions of the current BSA lightweights.

With minor revisions, the customer Goldie continued until 1963 and was still being raced decades later.

Triumph Tiger Cub

Triumph's Tiger Cub was designed unashamedly to appeal to those who admired the company's sporting twins. With the hand of master stylist Edward Turner much in evidence, they offered an attractive alternative to a string of lightweights mostly powered by proprietary Villiers two-strokes. The 'Baby Bonnies' provided a desirable apprenticeship on two wheels for a generation of youths, and a ride-to-work bike with style. After 1960, when learners were restricted to bikes of less than 250cc, the Cub's appeal was enormously enhanced.

Although by the 1950s Triumph was very much associated with twins, thanks to its trend-setting Speed Twin and later derivatives, prewar much of its production had centred on sports singles. The first postwar single was the much more mundane Terrier – a 150cc machine very much aimed at the commuter market, which Triumph had tended to foresake in recent years. Looking much like the Cub that followed, the Terrier was designed as a baby version of the twins, taking all their styling cues, and was distinguished from many of its cheaply made competitors by an air of completeness and quality. Its weakest points were rear suspension by plungers, and a big end assembly that proved rather too short-lived. The engine was built in unit with a four-speed gearbox and enclosed in a streamlined casing.

The first Cub, the T20, was simply a larger version of the Terrier, using the same plunger frame and cycle parts. A weak area of the frame that persisted for years was the swan-necked and unsupported headstock. This was braced by the tank, which was constructed in such a way that a stiffening tunnel ran from headstock to just forward of the seat. If this was replaced with another type of tank, the frame could prove extremely flimsy.

Apart from an increase in bore and stroke to give a capacity of 199cc, the engine unit changed little from the near-square unit of the original Terrier, including some irritating foibles. In particular, it was difficult to change the chain, and a new sprocket meant major dismantling, while the alternator inside the primary chaincase would prove the seat of many an electrical problem. The clutch and big end had led to many dissatisfied Terrier buyers, and had had to be redesigned.

The Cub's bottom end was changed in 1956 to a plain bearing, but this also proved troublesome, especially in the hands of novice riders who would rev the engine before it had warmed up properly, or economical owners who neglected to change the oil frequently enough. Big end life in such circumstances was depressingly short, and Triumph suffered many warranty claims before this fundamental flaw was sorted out.

Triumph's diminutive 200 provided an attractive alternative to a host of two-stroke lightweights. With styling borrowed from its bigger brothers, and a four-stroke single engine, it was the passport to two wheels for many a learner motorcyclist in the late 1950s and into the 1960s and beyond.

The frame was modified in 1957 gaining a swinging-arm rear suspension with twin shock absorber units. A competition (off-road) version called the T20C appeared that year, sporting a high-level exhaust and modified wheels and suspension. The basic styling remained that of the larger Triumphs, with four-bar tank badge, nacelle enclosing the headlamp, instruments and upper fork legs.

There were numerous styling and mechanical changes over the years. Variations on a theme included sports and off-road versions, while in 1966 the Bantam Cub appeared – a hybrid with the baby Triumph engine in a BSA Bantam frame. The last Tiger Cub was the Super Cub, launched in 1967 and dropped a year later. But the Cubs had laid the seeds for its replacement by becoming the inspiration for the 250cc BSA C15, which appeared a decade later.

Triumph's nacelle was a familiar styling feature. As well as rotary switchgear and the speedometer, it incorporated a gear position indicator needle linked to the gearbox via a rack-and-pinion mechanism and cable.

Triumph Tiger Cub (1959)

Years in production: 1956-68 (all model variations)

Engine type: single-cylinder ohv four-stroke

Capacity: 199cc

Power: 14bhp @ 6500rpm

Carburettor: Amal

Tyres (front/rear): 3¼ ×17in

Weight: 230lb

Top speed: 60mph

Panther M120

For many years the biggest single-cylinder motorcycle in the world, Panther's 650 sloper announced that fact with a deep, lazy engine beat, which was said to 'fire every other lamppost'. With enormous torque and incredible economy, it was ideally suited to pulling the enormous sidecars that formed budget family transport.

The Model 120 was the final product of P&M of Cleckheaton, Yorkshire – the factory that had built its first motorcycle at the beginning of the 20th century with the revolutionary idea of using a sloping engine, instead of the front portion of a conventional frame. From first to last, it was this concept that defined Panthers, with gradual concessions to the engine and suspension designs of the changing years.

By the 1930s the form of the big single Panther had pretty much settled, and the firm also survived through the lean early years of the decade, thanks to the excellent volume sales of the ultra-cheap Red Panther 250cc lightweight which sold for under £30.

After the war the machines that appeared bore a close resemblance to the prewar models. The Model 100 Panther for 1946 was a 600cc single with rigid frame and girder forks. It was ideally set up for economical sidecar use, with a fuel consumption in excess of 60 mpg.

The next year Dowty Oleomatic air-sprung telescopic forks were fitted – a form of front suspension that was very efficient when new, but gave problems when older as the seals wore. There were minor improvements to various parts of the bike until 1954 when a new, conventionally sprung fork was fitted, and a swinging-arm frame was adopted. Styling changes followed, and the rigid model was discontinued in 1957.

Handsome, solid and dependable, the 650cc Panther Model 120 was rarely seen in solo form; most performed sterling service as power for the family sidecar outfit.

The main news for 1958 was the development of the larger Model 120, which was closely based on the 600cc model, both bored and stroked. But that year's prototypes displayed a number of engine problems, largely a result of the increased stress and problems with Panther's unusual lubrication system. Based on a large sump cast into the front of the engine, this pumped oil up to the top of the engine, but return was hit-and-miss. With the more powerful, more stressed engine of the Model 120, the oil scavenging became less efficient and consumption became heavy.

The production bikes were substantially improved, and offered even lower fuel consumption – 70 mpg with a sidecar – than their predecessor. The Model 120 was ideally suited to sidecar use. In 1959 Panther's own sidecar chassis was an option – and this even included a towbar for a trailer.

The mode of progress of such an outfit was stately, but relaxing – once the machine had been started. The enormously heavy flywheels took considerable effort to get

Panther Model 120 (1959)

Years in production: 1959-66

Engine type: single-cylinder ohv four-stroke

Bore and stroke: 88 x 106mm

Capacity: 645cc

Compression ratio: 6.5:1

Power: 27bhp @ 4500rpm

Gearbox: Sturmey Archer three-speed

Tyres (front/rear): $3\frac{1}{2}$ x 19in/$3\frac{1}{2}$ x 19in (interchangeable)

Wheelbase: 59in

Turning circle: 19ft 6in

Weight: 168lb

spinning, especially with the engine's long stroke. To ease this, Panther fitted its own patented aid to the normal exhaust valve lifter. A small lever on the timing chest raised a ramp on the exhaust cam, lifting the valve partly off its seat, thus reducing the compression enough to allow the engine to spin more easily.

The simple, generally understressed big Panthers offered vintage values in a changing world. But sales of all Panther's range had been falling since the end of the 1950s, and by 1962 the firm was in receivership. An enlightened receiver kept them in production for a few years, mainly using up existing spares. But when difficulties arose obtaining major components – the separate Lucas Magdyno and Burman gearbox, which were by then virtually outmoded – there was no realistic way forward.

The last Panthers were built in 1966, although they remained on sale for at least a year after that. They were extremely cheap, but times had moved on and there was no longer any demand for the big sidecar outfit, as cheap cars took over that role and big bikes began the move towards becoming leisure vehicles.

Slogging power (below): the long stroke sloper engine possesses a legendary torque, despite its antiquated layout. The forward projecting casting is an oil reservoir, part of a near-vintage lubrication system. Despite such dated features, it was more the use of a separate gearbox and magneto that became unavailable that spelt the end of the big Panther, rather than any design shortcomings.

Manufacturers' badges from 1940–1959

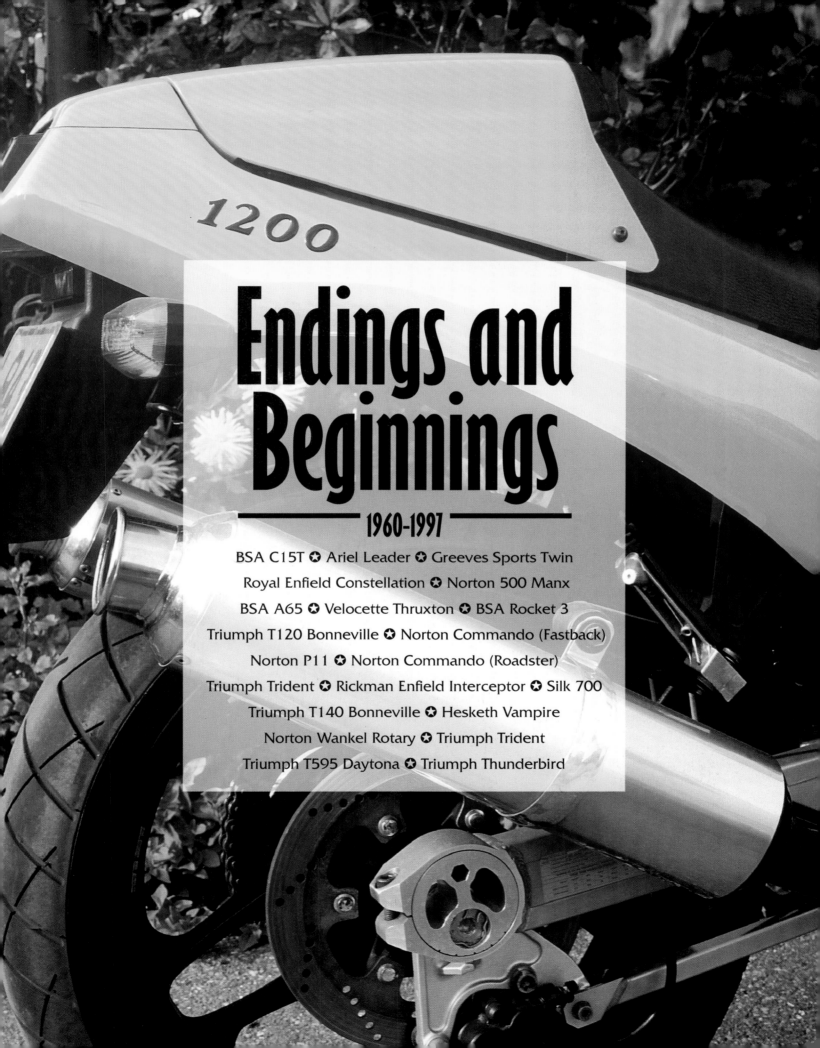

Endings and Beginnings

1960-1997

BSA C15T ✪ Ariel Leader ✪ Greeves Sports Twin

Royal Enfield Constellation ✪ Norton 500 Manx

BSA A65 ✪ Velocette Thruxton ✪ BSA Rocket 3

Triumph T120 Bonneville ✪ Norton Commando (Fastback)

Norton P11 ✪ Norton Commando (Roadster)

Triumph Trident ✪ Rickman Enfield Interceptor ✪ Silk 700

Triumph T140 Bonneville ✪ Hesketh Vampire

Norton Wankel Rotary ✪ Triumph Trident

Triumph T595 Daytona ✪ Triumph Thunderbird

Endings and Beginnings

As the 1960s dawned, they ushered in a new era in motorcycling – and a combination of powerful forces that would soon see the British industry reduced from a world leader to an also-ran, and finally to near-oblivion. And yet, during a decade that would see the creation of some of the best-loved British machines of all time, it was hard to spot where the downfall began. A third of million new machines were registered in 1959 and everything seemed to be booming. While the scooter and other continental imports had made significant inroads into British bike sales, it seemed as though there was still plenty of room in the market place for everyone.

On the face of it, Britain still had a thriving industry. Great names such as AJS, BSA, Matchless, Norton, Triumph and Velocette were still offering a wide range of singles and twins with their traditional qualities of, on the one hand, dependable economy, and on the other, sporting performance. There were exciting new models either recently launched, or soon to be announced, such as the radical Ariel Leader/Arrow, and new twins from Norton, BSA and Triumph. Such smaller independent concerns as Cotton, Greeves and DMW offered a wide range of budget models with two-stroke engines, mostly from the long-established Villiers factory, while similar models from Francis Barnett or James came with the backing of the major industry groups to which these names belonged.

The shadows on the horizon are easier to spot with hindsight. One was the introduction of the Mini car. Costing around the same as a top-of-the-range motorcycle or sidecar combination – chic and fun to drive, with it – it was the beginning of the end for bikes as basic transport. Another factor was the launch of the Honda Dream in 1959. Its quirky styling masked, for a time, the fact that here was a 250cc machine that could run rings around many machines twice its size and had an electric-starter, to boot. Against this beautifully engineered overhead-camshaft twin, the British industry was fielding machines powered by the basically sound, but low-powered Villiers two-strokes and the recently launched and badly flawed Norton Jubilee pushrod twin. In 1961 Honda would be followed by Yamaha and Suzuki, both concerns which rapidly began to establish themselves as major forces in racing as well as roadsters.

Motorcycling itself was attracting a bad press, with scare stories in the papers about the antics of rockers and rising accident rate that proved it was more than just media hype. The year 1960 saw the introduction of a limit on learner riders to machines of under 250cc, while insurance rates started to creep up, sure-fire factors in discouraging young riders from making a start.

By this time, the British industry consisted mainly of two large combines, the giant BSA-Triumph group (which also included Ariel and other famous names), based in the

The 1963 film The Leather Boys *(above) illustrated many of the problems which would come to bedevil the British bike industry over the next decade. Bikes were increasingly coming to be seen as a fringe pursuit with a questionable image, while the staple pushrod parallel twins were already looking dated when compared to developments abroad.*

Traditional factories such as the Ariel plant (below) photographed in the 1950s, relied on labour-intensive hand building. But the BSA Triumph group, which owned Ariel, were alive to the need for change, installing new lines and computer controls at the BSA factory in Small Heath, which made the factory one of the most modern in the world.

Midlands, and the lesser Associated Motorcycles (AMC), which included AJS, Francis Barnett, James, Matchless, and Norton, largely based in Plumstead, South London. There were plenty of small independents, too, such as Royal Enfield or Velocette, although many of the great names, for example Vincent, had already disappeared.

Whatever the cause of the British industry's troubles, it was certainly not just a lack of foresight. Both the major conglomerates had invested considerable sums in development throughout the 1950s and on into the 1960s. AMC retooled extensively in the 1950s and BSA spent a small fortune a decade later equipping its Small Heath plant with the latest assembly line technology, including state-of-the-art computer controlled production and spares.

Some of this investment was misguided, since it required heavy cash injections that the BSA Group could ill afford, while the very size of the group meant that management was unwieldy and tended to the bureaucratic. One symptom of this was the installation in 1967 of a central research and development facility for the whole group at Umberslade Hall, an attractive country estate near Solihull, equidistant from each of the main factories. The trouble with such an arrangement (besides being very costly in itself) was that it tended to create a situation in which R&D staff were remote from the problems of production, while traditional rivalries between the factories still existed.

AMC had no such capital to invest in new measures and witnessed their traditional customer base being eroded by degrees. The group's once proud heritage in road racing was largely behind it by the 1960s, with the rightly famed Manx Norton winning its last TT in 1961, while the privateer racers, the 350cc AJS 7R and 500cc Matchless G50, were phased out in the mid-60s. As far as the roadsters went, the days of the

traditional big single were virtually over, and, despite an enviable reputation for assembly and finish, the crunch came in 1966 against a background of falling sales. The Norton factory had previously had to be closed in 1962 and moved to London. Such rationalisation was too little, too late, and with funds having dried up, the company was acquired by the industrial group Manganese Bronze Holdings. At a stroke, Francis Barnett and James were no more. From that time until the late 1960s – when the original factory in Plumstead was closed and Norton was joined with Villiers in yet another industry amalgamation – only the bigger Nortons and Matchless models were made .

Many smaller factories were forced to close as a result of the Norton-Villiers merger, for Villiers was the last volume supplier of proprietary engines, and these were now cut off in a move to consolidate the engine supply for Norton-Villiers own project, the AJS Stormer scramblers. Of the important small independents, only Greeves had developed sufficiently to manufacture their own engines, and such names as Cotton and Dot were forced to look overseas, or fold, which eventually happened.

Another great name had disappeared in 1963, coincidentally the first year in which MOT tests were applied, initially for machines of over five years old. Ariel, as part of the BSA group had been moved from their Selly Oak factory to BSA's Small Heath plant, and ceased to be.

Final fling: the Norton Commando and Triumph Bonneville represented the ultimate development of an engine concept that could be traced back to before the war, although the innovative frame concept of the Commando in particular proved that there was still plenty of life in the old ideas.

The refusal of the workers at Triumph's old Meriden plant to accept redundancy culminated in a sit-in at the factory (left) and many months of unrest, after which new owners NVT were forced to accept defeat. Government funding helped the Meriden workers' co-operative to continue in production for several years in the late 1970s.

Great white hope (below): the Norton rotary was developed from one of the last projects of the old BSA research facility. Many years of steady development proved that the idea worked, and well enough to win races. But while the new Norton sold in small numbers to institutional users and enthusiasts, it was never able to achieve proper volume production and economies of scale.

The revamped Norton Villiers group started confidently with the appointment of a new chief designer and the development of a new model that would become a great name of the industry – the Commando.

Such new models were very necessary. The British industry's one-time confidence that the Japanese would confine themselves to small machines had been shattered by the arrival of the Honda 450 'Black Bomber' in 1965, and while this was never a best-seller, it paved the way for other larger machines from Japan. And by this time, it was also well known that Honda was working on the epoch-making 750 Four.

BSA-Triumph were in serious trouble. Almost all their new developments had failed to bring them the hoped for benefits, and many ageing models had been discontinued. But there were promising signs, too. In 1967 and 1968 the companies' sales efforts earned them Queen's Awards for Industry, while in 1968 the group announced its own new models, again to become legends. These were the Triumph Trident and BSA Rocket III – both derived, not so much from the group's new R&D headquarters, as an expedient reworking of the forty-year-old Triumph Speed Twin. Still, they were great bikes, that was the important thing, and were sorely needed.

Many of the major manufacturers' promising ideas had failed to make it into production. Of the smaller independents, Royal Enfield and Panther were already part of history, while Velocette was on its last set of wheels.

The launch of the first Japanese superbikes in 1969 hit the British bikes hard. Disastrous losses culminated in a rescue plan in 1972, which would merge BSA/Triumph with Norton Villiers to form Norton Villiers Triumph (NVT), as duly happened in 1973. There were some interesting footnotes, however. On the racing side, in 1972 Norton entered into a famous association with John Player cigarettes, which would go on to win fame and glory for the resulting JPN team. The same year, the little AJS Stormer, and the rights to the name, were sold off to former development engineer Fluff Brown, who continued to make small numbers of the FB-AJS off-roaders.

Great survivor (above): the Villiers-engined AJS Stormer was one of the last machines from the old AMC combine in the 1960s. Now updated and still made by former development engineer Fluff Brown, it represents the kind of enthusiastic small-volume production that survived the demise of the major manufacturers.

But the biggest side effect of the merger came with the proposed reorganisation of the factories. This would have resulted in closure of the old Triumph plant at Meriden, Coventry, but the 1750 workers took exception to this and undertook a sit-in. After a year-and-a-half, during which NVT was unable to get access to the Trident parts held in the factory, the model had to be effectively discontinued. With falling sales of the Commando, NVT's Norton plant virtually gave up production after 1976, concentrating on the assembly of small numbers of mopeds using Italian engines, and small trail bikes based on Yamaha components. They moved to a new, smaller factory in Shenstone, Staffs, after 1978.

The great survivor, somewhat perversely, was Meriden, where after a long-drawn-out struggle, the government finally stepped in with funding to start the Meriden Co-operative in 1975. The Co-op would continue building what they knew best, Triumph twins, as well as continuing their own efforts to assemble machines from overseas parts.

Many smaller independents continued, including notables such as Rickman, Weslake, Seeley, Spondon and Silk. Such companies made an interesting range of specials, often including frames for Japanese machines, for this was an area where British expertise was still acknowledged. But such efforts were virtually doomed to remain small, for by this time most of the major component suppliers that had supported the British industry with parts such as electrics, carburettors, wheels, tanks and mudguards were themselves disappearing or diversifying.

This did not mean that there were not people prepared to try. In the late 1970s and early 1980s Lord Alexander Hesketh captured the public imagination with news of the latest British 'world-beater', a machine built to the highest standards and designed to take on the best foreign competition. It was the sort of good news which the industry needed – for in 1982, after a long struggle, the Meriden co-op folded, and the last remaining Bonnevilles were now being assembled in small numbers in Devon.

Hesketh's efforts failed, and from this time on, the British bike was virtually a cottage industry. It was condemned to depend on imports of foreign components for such rebirths as a new 'Matchless G50', which used the Austrian Rotax engine, although the burgeoning interest in older 'classics' helped to keep specialist frame-builders and skilled engineers in business.

The one obvious ray of hope during the 1980s was Norton, the inheritor of one of BSA's own 'world-beaters' using the new rotary engine technology. It was a story that could have been designed to appeal to the British psyche, as the little underdogs laboured against all the odds to produce a model that was not only successful in its own terms but actually managed a string of famous racing wins to demonstrate what might have been, if only. Sadly, it was a case of too little, too late, and Norton all but disappeared in a welter of accusation and counter-accusation of financial mismanagement.

And so it all might have ended, except for Triumph. Virtually unnoticed for several years, and deliberately avoiding the kind of publicity that Norton and Hesketh had courted, the new owner of the remnants of the old Meriden assets had set out to make a range of machines which would genuinely merit the 'world-beater' tag. Accepting the new era of design and the new commercial realities of the late 1980s and 1990s, the reborn Triumph had almost nothing to do with the old, except the name and the loyalty which that could command. Starting with a clean sheet and an open chequebook, it was the creation of a single entrepreneur – the kind of figure that had helped to create the industry a century before. But above all, Triumph is proof that the skills that helped to make the British bike the envy of the world still exist. As all those behind the mergers and start-ups of the last 20 years of the industry had hoped, it is simply a matter of providing the proper environment in which those skills can be expressed.

BSA C15T

BSA's lightweight singles of the 1960s came to symptomise much of what was wrong with the British industry at the time. Yet they provided transport for thousands of young riders, and the trials versions can also be said to have helped to usher in the modern era of off-road sport, while being very successful in their own right.

BSA had acquired the Triumph marque at the start of the 1950s, and while the company had been rightly famous for its lightweights in the past, those that appeared towards the end of the decade owed far more to Triumph than to BSA.

Chief among them was the 1958 C15 Star. A 250cc four-stroke, long a popular BSA configuration, its pushrod single-cylinder engine was almost totally derived from the 200cc Triumph Tiger Cub, albeit with an upright cylinder in place of the Cub's inclined unit. The Cub itself was derived from the earlier 150cc Terrier, and both had proved unreliable, with a weak bottom end, among other failings.

Even so, in its BSA incarnation the new model seemed both up-to-date and sophisticated, with its light weight and sophisticated electrics setting it apart from the competition. And with learners restricted to 250s from 1960, it was one of the most attractive alternatives – if one discounted the Honda twins that appeared in 1961.

As with its Triumph predecessors, the C15 and its derivatives suffered from minor electrical problems, oil leaks and somewhat complicated maintenance routines. But it went well enough and was mainly reliable. The SS80 sports version, which appeared in 1961, was faster, while the 350 version, the B40, offered more power and appealed to army buyers as well as the general public. In the mid 1960s a similar engine layout was seen in the shape of the 75cc Beagle and 50cc Ariel Pixie, two fatally flawed attempts by the BSA Group to launch an ultra-lightweight.

Over the years there were countless variations on the same theme, including sports and off-road versions, while the basic engine was stretched to 441 and finally 499cc. The engine even found its way back to Triumph, to power the street-scrambler-styled singles of the late 1960s and early 1970s. The last of BSA's C15 derivatives was the B50, built until 1973. Even after this, the specialist company CCM of Bolton built their own derivative of the B50 for off-road competition throughout the 1970s and on into 1981.

Off-road sport was long a speciality of BSA. In the postwar era, the 350 and

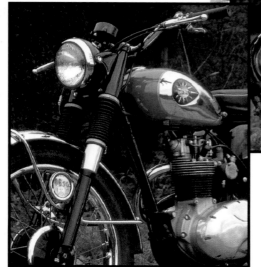

Despite its serious competition aspirations, the 250 still carried full road equipment (left) including electrics by the unreliable and unloved energy-transfer system.

Superficially the same unit as the roadster, the trials bike's all-alloy engine (left) concealed a host of minor modifications, as well as a set of gearbox ratios more suited to off-road use. The iron-barrelled engine was derived from Triumph's Terrier and Tiger Cub, and itself spawned a whole generation of derivatives.

Relatively lightweight, with taut handling and good suspension, BSA's C15T capitalised on the virtues of the roadster to produce a trials bike that helped to usher in the modern era.

500cc Gold Stars had been enormously successful trials and scrambles mounts, but the company correctly anticipated the modern era and its shift towards lighter, more manageable machines. The lightweight, unit-construction C15 offered a great deal of potential, and the competition shop soon developed works specials that were ridden with a great deal of success, notably by expert rider and BSA employee Brian Martin.

Production versions followed the C15S scrambler and C15T trials machine. Superficially similar to the roadsters, there were in fact numerous differences, which included frames, wheels and suspension, as well as a host of engine modifications. The gear ratios were of course specially chosen for off-road, while the electrics used the so-called energy-transfer system. This did away with a battery, saving weight, but was notoriously problematic.

Even so, the true competition bikes succeeded famously. On the 441cc derivative, Jeff Smith won the world motocross championship in 1964 and 1965. It was the design's finest hour.

BSA C15T (1960)

Years in production: 1958-73 (all variations), 1959-65 (C15T)

Engine type: single-cylinder ohv four-stroke

Bore and stroke: 67 x 70 mm

Capacity: 247cc

Compression ratio: 7:1

Power: 15bhp @ 5000rpm

Carburettor: Amal Monobloc

Exhaust: high level

Weight: 275lb

Top speed: 75mph

Ariel Leader

Ariel Leader (1961)

Years in production: 1958-65

Engine type: parallel twin two-stroke

Bore and stroke: 54 x 54mm (48.5 x 54mm)

Capacity: 249cc (199.5cc)

Power: 17.5bhp @ 6750rpm

Carburettor: Amal Monobloc

Tyres (front/rear): $3\frac{1}{4}$ x 16in/ $3\frac{1}{4}$ x 16in

Top speed: 73mph

One of the most technically innovative offerings of the postwar years of the British industry, Ariel's futuristic two-stroke was designed from scratch for mass transport. As part of the giant BSA group, Ariel had been manufacturing its traditional four-stroke singles, the Square Four, and a version of the BSA 650 twin when, in 1955, BSA decided to turn the entire resource of the factory over to a revolutionary new design offering low maintenance and full weather protection.

In doing so they may have been influenced by the enormous boom in sales of (mainly imported) scooters, although the machine that was eventually produced was far from a traditional scooter. Instead, it was a full-size 250cc motorcycle, albeit with small (16in) wheels. It was built entirely of pressed steel, which ideally lent itself to mass production, and offered tremendous strength. Unfortunately, the high initial cost of the tooling meant that it cost a great deal to get into production, while it was expensive to modify the design.

Not that there was anything inherently wrong with the final design of veteran Val Page, the man behind some of the most successful products of the British industry. Assisted by Bernard Knight, every aspect embodied sound logical thinking. It was based on a strong box beam that contributed to the excellent handling, and which, by acting as a low-slung fuel reservoir, helped to keep the centre of gravity down. The trailing-link forks with dampers concealed inside the legs worked extremely efficiently despite their odd appearance.

The engine hung below the main beam, and was designed as an integrated unit. A 250cc parallel twin with 180 degree firing interval, the cylinders were angled at 45 degrees to help keep the weight low slung. There were a number of similarities between the engine design and that of the German Adler, which went out of production just before Ariel launched their Leader. But while the engine shared several important dimensions, there were so many differences and developments that it could hardly be called a simple copy.

When the Leader appeared in 1958 it offered a complete package, with integral fairing and windscreen, and a dummy 'petrol tank' that was actually a luggage compartment, plus a host of practical and

On the Leader the 6-inch headlamp was housed in the fairing. On the Arrow (above), it is supported by extensions forwards from the tank.

844 VVX

decorative extras. But despite its practical appeal and initially good response, many traditional motorcycle customers were turned off by its styling, while others were wooed by the appeal of the cheaper scooter and the revolutionary Mini.

Its cost may also have been too high, and in an attempt to appeal to the more sporting motorcyclist, as well as offer a cheaper alternative, the Leader was redesigned as the unfaired Arrow, launched in 1960. Again, the styling was odd – the engine was never intended to be on view and the front fork and mudguard appeared rather clumsy. But the machine was lighter, with a decent performance, and it was much cheaper – as it needed to be in a competitive market.

Ariel's entire production was devoted to the new range, and in a good month well over 1000 were produced. Tuning experiments upped the power of a works-developed model enough for it to come seventh in the lightweight TT, and the position looked promising.

For 1961 a new cylinder head improved the power of the standard machines, and a super sports version, the Golden Arrow, was also launched. But the reliability and practicality which Ariel had hoped for were not what they should have been. Starting could be poor, the gear change was rough, and some maintenance jobs were tricky. Two-stroke technology of the time also meant that while the engine was quick, it was often smoky.

The construction of the beam frame, complete with dummy tank, is clear to see in the unfaired Arrow (above), introduced as a more sporting model. The trailing-link forks gave good handling, but the unconventional appearance and clumsy mudguard did not endear them to sporting riders.

In 1963 the Ariel factory was absorbed into the main BSA plant. With cleaner, more practical machines appearing from Japan, even the launch in 1964 of a 200cc version, could not mask the fact that a total production run of some 17,000 was much too few. Production ended in 1965, and with it the Ariel name, although it was resurrected for two spectacularly unsuccessful BSA-designed lightweights, the Pixie and the Ariel 3, over the next few years.

The fully enclosed Ariel Leader was introduced to fill a need for mass transport. Modern features included integral fairing and screen, and there were optional panniers, indicators and many other convenient accessories.

Greeves Sports Twin

Built by one of Britain's smallest manufacturers, Greeves lightweights were true individuals with an all-round quality that often put to shame the offerings from the major motorcycle factories.

The company took its name from one man, Bert Greeves, but it was really the product of two partners. The other half was Greeves' cousin Preston Derry Cobb, paralysed from birth but very much an active partner when they went into business shortly after World War II. In those early days the product was a motorised invalid carriage, and the company was called Invacar.

The invalid carriages sold well and established a firm foundation for the factory, which was based in Thundersley, near Benfleet in Essex. Although small, and reliant on proprietary engines that were produced by Villiers, the factory possessed its own foundry and very soon became expert in the new technology of fibreglass moulding. The invalid cars also featured some innovative design, notably suspension by rubber bushes that acted as self-damping springs when they twisted.

By the early 1950s Bert Greeves, an enthusiastic motorcyclist and no mean off-road rider, was able to indulge his interests by constructing a prototype scrambler (motocross) machine. After this had been thoroughly proved in competition, production versions of both an off-road machine and a roadster appeared in 1954. Using Villiers or British Anzani engines, and front and rear suspension based on the invalid cars' rubber units, the frames illustrated another Greeves innovation. In place of the normal tubular fabricated front section and steering head was a

single aluminium alloy casting. This was an enormously strong H-section beam into which was cast a steel top tube and lugs for the engine mountings. Other fittings included the proprietary electrics and British Hub brakes used by a host of other small manufacturers.

It was the frame and front forks, which used short leading links, that really set Greeves aside from the rest. Despite their unconventional appearance, they offered superb handling on or off the road. For a time public resistance to the design meant that Greeves made some conventionally framed machines, too, but when experienced competition rider Brian Stonebridge joined the company in the mid 1950s, Greeves started to make a name for itself with an incredible series of giant-killing demonstrations, which vindicated their unconventional ideas.

Roadster production had centred on a range of modest lightweight twins, mainly powered by Villiers 250 and

Greeves 32DC (1961)

Years in production: 1956-63
   (with engine variations)

Engine type: 180 degree parallel
   twin two-stroke (Villiers 3T)

Bore and stroke: 57 x 63.5 mm

Capacity: 324cc

Compression ratio: 8.7:1

Power: 17bhp @ 5250rpm

Carburettor: Villiers 25mm

Tyres (front/rear): 20in/18in

Weight: 270lb

Top speed: 74mph

325cc units, after some early Anzani-engined models. By the 1960s the Sports Twins had become probably the best of their kind, thanks to Greeves handling and quality build. An indication of the regard in which they were held was their adoption as police bikes.

Numbers were inevitably small, however, with only around 300 racers and a few thousand roadsters appearing throughout the 1960s. As the decade wore on, Greeves fell victim to a number of pressures. First its engine supplier Villiers was taken over, and then the British market saw the first influx of sophisticated Japanese lightweights. Invacar, too, fell victim to the changing times. It was taken over in 1973, but in any case government support for specialist invalid cars ceased shortly afterwards. The last Greeves roadsters had left the factory in 1968, but they had designed a new motocrosser around their own single-cylinder 360cc engine. Its derivatives stayed in production until 1978, although a disastrous factory fire in 1976 was really the end of Greeves as a volume manufacturer.

Competition machines (above) ran in parallel with the roadsters. Typical of the breed was this 246cc Model 24MDS scrambler, modified to take part in the 1963 ISDT.

With the company's distinctive alloy front-beam frame and forks, and a finish in Moorland Blue, the Sports Twin in either 250 or 325cc form was one of Greeves' best loved roadsters. Despite its reliance on proprietary engine, electrics and brakes, it offered better handling and comfort than other Villiers-powered lightweights, plus a pedigree that was proven in competition.

Royal Enfield Constellation

Big parallel twins may have been the staple fare of the British industry in the late 1950s and 60s, but there were plenty of variations on the theme. With a character all its own, Royal Enfield's twin offered one of several alternatives to BSA/Triumph conformity, and was for several years the largest of its kind.

Royal Enfield's first postwar twin appeared in 1948 and owed more to the company's singles than to the competition. A 500cc engine in the 350 single's swinging-arm frame, it featured separate heads and barrels that improved cooling and serviceability at some cost to strength, while the crankcase incorporated a cast-in oil container at the rear. Ignition was by battery, coil and distributor, and although the Albion gearbox was a separate unit, it was rigidly bolted to the rear of the engine. It was

rather unimaginatively called the 500 Twin.

A few years later the 1953 700cc Meteor went one better than the rival 650s by offering what was effectively a doubled-up 350 single. Technically it offered some advanced features, such as a diecast cylinder head, and a double-sided alloy front brake. This included sophisticated adjustment and balancing arrangements, and although only 6in in diameter was initially a good stopper.

Design changes for both models followed, including such seemingly retrograde steps as a switch to magneto and dynamo electrics. Major changes to the engine, lubrication system and cycle parts resulted in the 1956 Super Meteor – an excellent all-rounder – while the 500 Twin was similarly improved. A year later, with the Vincent V-twin already gone (and the Ariel Square Four being phased out), the big Enfield achieved the distinction of being the largest capacity twin on the market.

The 700cc Constellation was launched in the United States in 1957, but first appeared in Britain in 1958, along

Royal Enfield Constellation (1961)

Years in production: 1958-63

Engine type: 360 degree parallel twin ohv four-stroke

Bore and stroke: 70 x 90 mm

Capacity: 692cc

Compression ratio: 8:1

Power: 51bhp @ 6250rpm

Carburettors: twin Amal Monoblocs

Tyres (front/rear): 3¼ x 18in/3½ x 17in

Weight: 403lb

Top speed: 116mph

Another classic Royal Enfield feature, the cast-alloy casquette (below) combined instrument housing, top yoke and light shell in one unit.

Beefy, purposeful and powerful, in its day the 'Connie' was the biggest British twin.

with a new and much lighter 500, the Meteor Minor. With new engine castings, the 'Connie' was a sportier design with a very robust bottom end, hot cams and, initially, a single racing Amal TT carburettor. With a suitably tuned cylinder head, the resulting bike was a real road-burner capable of well over 110mph. On test, it bettered 115mph.

The racing carb disappeared in favour of twin Monoblocs in 1959, but the bike was still fast – although it soon gained a reputation for fragility, while the front brake was inadequate for the power and speed. In fact, there were a number of niggles, which meant that the model never achieved the popularity of machines such as the Triumph twins, despite its theoretical advantages and better acceleration.

To counter complaints of heavy vibration, the crankshaft was redesigned. The rather weak clutch was altered in 1961, and there were a number of styling changes. This became the ultimate example of the 'Connie', because in 1963 Enfield launched the even larger 750 Interceptor (actually a 736cc design) while the Constellation was mainly relegated to sidecar duty before production ceased that year. The 750 twins only lasted a few years more. With the company suffering from the financial malaise of much of the industry, production suffered a short gap before the model bowed out at the start of the 1970s.

Norton 500 Manx

As a company, Norton came to be dominated by the demands of racing, and for many years a wide gulf separated their bread-and-butter products from the exotics developed in the race shop. While the policy might not have been ideal for commercial success, it nevertheless produced one of the most phenomenally effective racers of all time – the Manx Norton single.

Finning that completely enclosed the bevel drive shaft (left) is a characteristic of the later, short-stroke models. The stiff crankcase in Elektron magnesium alloy extends right up to the bottom fins.

The Manx Norton was also one of the supreme examples of the value of constant development, in the hands of race engineer Joe Craig whose meticulous experiments kept squeezing more and more power out of the design as each season passed.

The Manx was itself a development from the single overhead-cam International racers. A dohc layout had been tried as early as 1937, with a larger cambox in which a gear train operated twin camshafts bearing directly on a pair of valve 'pushers' in contact with the valve stems. Inspired partly by experiments at rivals Velocette, this design was not immediately successful, although it reappeared in 1938 with revised engine dimensions and supposedly phenomenal power output.

The Manx name was first used late in 1939, but in 1940 all racing efforts ceased. The name appeared once again in 1946 before September's amateur Manx Grand Prix, where several entrants rode that season's new racer. With an engine based on the prewar International, the dohc cambox was used, while the machines sported the new telescopic front forks tried on the works bikes in 1938. Performance, however, was disappointing, partly as a result of the low-octane 'Pool' petrol then in use.

Gradually, a steady process of development began to pay dividends. In 1948 a twin leading-shoe brake appeared, and with 112mph potential, it was needed. By 1950, with 120mph performance, it was essential.

The year 1950 saw the most significant leap in Manx technology, with the adoption of the new 'Featherbed' frame designed in Ireland by the McCandless brothers and Artie Bell. The new frame and suspension were a quantum leap for motorcycling in general, and gave Norton a massive edge over the competition. Its name was coined by rider Harold Daniell, enthusing about its comfort.

After a triumphant debut in the hands of Geoff Duke in April, the Featherbed Nortons went on to win a double hat trick at the TT, the first of many major wins. In 1951 both the 500 and 350 were listed as production racers – virtually identical to the works machines, the only significant differences between the two models being the engine size.

In 1953 the engines were redesigned with a much shorter stroke for improved revs, and many more wins ensued, despite the sophistication of the mainly Italian multi-cylinder competition. In 1954 streamlining was tested, resulting in yet more wins, but it was becoming clear that time was running out for the antiquated technology. Norton 'officially' withdrew from Grand Prix racing at the end of the season, although they continued to support works entries, and rivals Moto Guzzi continued to race single cylinders with considerable success until 1957.

The factory continued to develop the Manx, and gained many more wins, while the production models soldiered on as the mainstay of privateer competition for many years. Then, in 1961, Norton scored an amazing double hat trick at the TT – although most of the Italian makers were not competing that year. But the works efforts were switching to a new model, the Domiracer, which made its debut at that same event. It was effectively the model's swan song, although private enthusiasts developed and raced them for many more years. The last batch appeared in 1962, the year in which Norton works in Birmingham's Bracebridge Street closed, and the factory moved in with AMC in Plumstead, London.

Norton 500 Manx (1962)

Years in production: 1946-53 (long-stroke) 1953-62 (short-stroke)

Engine type: double overhead-cam single-cylinder four-stroke

Bore and stroke: 79.6 x100mm (1946-53), 86 x 85.6 (1953-62)

Capacity: 499cc

Compression ratio: 9.75:1

Power: 50bhp @ 7200rpm

Carburettors: 1½in Amal GP

Tyres (front/rear): 3 x 19in /3½ x 19in

Wheelbase: 56in

Top speed: 150mph (depending on gearing)

Light, purposeful and developed to the pitch of sophistication, the late Manx Norton epitomises the British racing single at its best, although newer designs had shown that similar performance could be achieved with far less fussy multi-cylinder engines. The full-loop double-cradle 'Featherbed' frame set the standard for more than two decades.

BSA A65

Along with its 500cc cousin, the A50, the problems that beset the A65 typify much of what went wrong with BSA towards the end of the company. The machines attracted a poor reputation for reliability and spares back up in particular, which helped to put the final nails in the coffin of a large part of the British industry. And yet the design had its good points, for with modification the engine unit proved itself in that most demanding of competition fields – sidecar racing – while surviving, hard-working bikes have clocked up tens of thousands of trouble-free miles.

By the 1960s BSA had become part of a large conglomerate with diverse interests. There had been a concerted effort to introduce new management systems, and there was an on-going drive to attract sales in the all-important American market. Despite the popularity of the existing 650cc twins, these were perceived as being of an increasingly antiquated design, which was losing out against the competition from Triumph in particular.

The new models were developed quickly, and many of their problems were the kind that a longer testing period would have ironed out. On the face of it, though, the new 650 offered promise, being more sophisticated and lighter than its A10-based predecessors. In place of their nuts-and-bolts separate engine, gearbox, magneto and dynamo, the engine

was a unit-construction design with fashionable 'power egg' streamlined styling and an alternator. Only a single carburettor was fitted, but with almost square dimensions, the engine promised to be free-revving, with room for an efficient combustion chamber design.

It was perhaps surprising, therefore, that it initially offered less power than the top-of-the-range A10-based machine, the Rocket Gold Star, although as the model was developed it became clear that there was much more available. The frame and forks were similar to the duplex cradle unit of the late A10s, but the geometry was changed to suit smaller wheels, and the bike was much more compact overall. The handling was generally quite good, although the rather crude damping of the front forks sometimes found the going tough.

When the A65 and smaller A50 were launched in 1962, they appeared to have plenty going for them. The styling fell into line with the clean, but rather lumpen BSA look of the period, with a weak point being the awkwardly large side panels, which extended forward, supposedly to tidy up the space behind the engine. The performance was not bad, with strong acceleration and a reasonable 100mph or so top speed – and the fuel economy was good.

The problems soon appeared, however. The engines were prone to vibration, but much more seriously, the main bearings self-destructed at depressingly low mileages, often blocking the oil pump and wrecking the engine. Oil leaks were common and the primary drive chain was also prone to rapid wear.

This did not prevent an A50 from taking Gold in the 1962 ISDT, while for the public, the A65 was soon offered in higher performance versions with sportier styling, higher and higher compression ratios, and latterly, twin carburettors. One such machine, the 650 Lightning, even managed to win a production race in 1965. For the American market initially, there were many variants, including scramblers.

'Power-egg' styling was a popular fashion in the 1960s, and the 650 BSA unit was perhaps the definitive version. All functions in the unit engine were smoothly faired in behind streamlined alloy casings.

BSA A65 (1966)

Years in production: 1962-72 (all A65 variants) 1966-68 (Spitfire models)

Engine type: twin-cylinder ohv four-stroke

Bore and stroke: 75 x 74mm

Capacity: 654cc

Compression ratio: 10 5:1 (Spitfire MkII)

Power: 54bhp @ 4500rpm (Spitfire MkII)

Gearbox: four-speed

Weight: 383lb (Spitfire MkII)

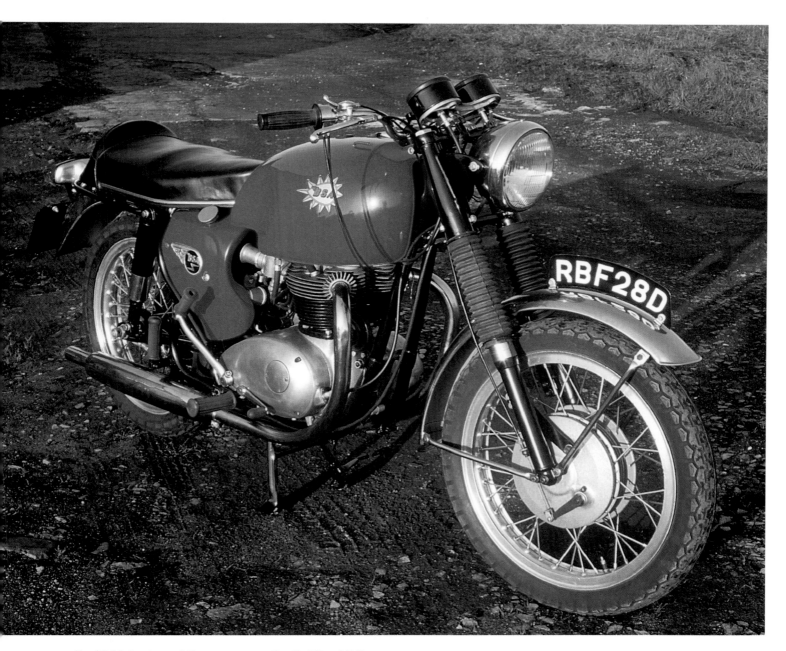

By 1966 the top of the range was the Spitfire MkII, which sported many racing fittings, such as close-ratio gears, a larger front brake and fibreglass tank. It was light and fast, with 120 mph within reach, and thanks to a new front fork, handled well. The introduction of 12 volt electrics was an improvement that benefited the whole range. But the problems were still there, as the awesome levels of vibration which were produced by sustained high speed running testified.

Much production was still aimed at the US market, and in 1967 BSA won an export award. The American market dictated many styling changes, which were less popular for the home market, such as high-rise bars and smaller tanks for several models.

There were several attempts at curing the engines' basic problems, but none that really succeeded, and from 1970 on, this flawed power unit gained a frame with problems of its own. This was the oil-in-frame unit, in which a large diameter backbone doubled as the oil tank. A similar design was adopted by Triumph, and although both handled well,

Handsome in a beefy way, the A65 eschewed the nuts-and-bolts looks of its predecessors in favour of a rounded, all-enclosed styling. With a highly-tuned, but fragile, engine, it offered true sports bike performance and the handling to exploit it.

they were so designed that the seat height precluded them being ridden comfortably by anyone who was much under six feet tall.

The model soldiered on until 1972, despite BSA's growing financial difficulties. By this time the seat height had been reduced to a much more workable level, handling was excellent and even the vibration seemed to have decreased. Sadly it was too late, and the A65 became a victim of BSA's need to make cuts.

There is a postscript, for a solution to the main-bearing problem had been proposed while developing the factory racers in 1966-7, but never adopted. After the model had been discontinued, ex-BSA workers offered this as an after-market conversion, consisting of a new set of main bearings an optional new oil pump and clutch modification.

Velocette Thruxton

The Thruxton Velo was the final development of Velocette's pushrod single – a machine that in essence dated back to the mid 1930s. Despite its simple and in many ways antiquated layout, this was a genuine 100mph machine, which could top 110 and still sip fuel at an astonishingly low rate through its massive racing carburettor.

Thruxton is the name of a race track in Hampshire – one of the many wartime airfields that found a new use during the 1950s. Racing at Thruxton centred on the endurance marathon for production machines, the 500-miler. The bikes had to be substantially catalogue models and the entries

were shared between two riders who took turn and turn about. Over the years many British stars shone in the event, including Dave Croxford, Percy Tait, Ray Pickrell and Paul Smart. Machines that achieved great things there included the racing bersion of the Triumph Bonneville, to which the event also gave its name, the BSA-Triumph threes, the John Player Norton Commandos – and the Velocette.

Velocette singles evolved slowly over the years. Their basic formula was laid down by the 1934 250cc MOV, with the camshaft mounted high up and the pushrods kept as short as possible, while their narrow crankcase, slimline clutch and outboard chain run dated back to the early vintage days. Larger capacities and shorter strokes followed over the years, and by the late 1950s the machine had evolved into the 350cc Viper and 500cc Venom.

These Velocettes had a sporting image and performance, and on 18–19 March a Clubman's Venom

The ultimate sports pushrod engine (right): tuning the Thruxton included a special head with extra large valves and a down-draught inlet port. This was matched to an enormous Amal GP carburettor that required special cut-aways in the tanks. Yet the engine was enormously flexible – there were only four ratios in the gearbox – and capable of astonishing fuel economy.

equipped with Velocette's own sports options and a full fairing set out to challenge the 24-hour speed record. After circulating the Monthléry speed bowl near Paris in the hands of a team of eight riders for a day and a night, it achieved an outstanding success. First the twelve-hour record fell at more than 104 mph, then the twenty four-hour record went at an average speed of 100 mph-plus – an enduring record.

In 1964 the high-cam Velo reached its ultimate development. The performance of the Clubman's Venom at Thruxton led to the makers offering a performance kit that included a special head with 2in inlet valve and an enormous Amal Grand Prix carburettor, plus oil and petrol tanks cut away to suit. For the following year, Velocette offered the Thruxton model with this kit, racing seat and footrests, swept-back exhaust and a twin-leading shoe alloy front brake.

Although the 1965 500-miler was held on an alternative circuit, the Velocettes dominated the race, with Dave Dixon and Joe Dunphy ahead at the last. The model soon found favour with sporting riders, for it was a genuine tuned roadster and was well able to cope with everyday use, despite being a fussy starter.

Its finest moment came in 1967, the year of the first Isle of Man Production TT. In the 500 class, Neil Kelly took the race at just under 90mph, as well as the fastest lap at over 91 mph. Fellow rider Keith Heckles was second.

Only a little more than 1200 Thruxtons were built, although the relative ease of converting a Venom meant that there were several more replicas constructed by private owners. In 1969 the ignition system had to be modified to coil ignition, as the traditional magneto had been phased out by Lucas. This was effectively the factory's swan song, for it bowed to commercial pressure in 1971, still a genuine family firm after 66 years.

Production racer: in 1967 the Thruxton dominated the inaugural Production TT, taking first, second and fastest lap. It was capable of more than 110mph and had proven endurance, having broken the 24-hour record.

Velocette Venom Thruxton (1967)

Years in production: 1965-71

Engine type: high-camshaft ohv four-stroke single

Bore and stroke: 86 x 86mm

Capacity: 499cc

Compression ratio: 9.2:1

Power: 41-47bhp @ 6200rpm

Carburettor: Amal GP

Tyres (front/rear): 3 x 19in/3¼ x 19in

Wheelbase: 54¾in

Top speed: 110mph

BSA Rocket 3

The late 1960s ushered in the age of the superbikes – machines with technical specifications and performances much superior to anything that had gone before. And although the bikes that really gave form to the name were Japanese, both BSA's and Triumph's triples were among the most important of the pioneers.

As part of the same manufacturing group, the BSA Rocket 3 and the slightly later Triumph Trident were based on the same original concept, although the differences between them went well beyond the name on the tank.

The original concept dated back to the early 1960s, when designers Bert Hopwood and Doug Hele realised that it would be quite simple to graft an extra cylinder on to the 500cc Triumph twin, producing a 750cc three-cylinder engine. The advantage of such a layout, apart from the increased capacity, would be that the inherent balance of a triple would result in a much smoother power delivery.

However, nothing was done with the idea for several years, until the company's board members were told of Honda's plans to produce a 750cc four-cylinder machine. A prototype was hastily put into production, and within a year it was developing a healthy 58bhp for a weight not much greater than the contemporary Triumph Bonneville twin.

To save time, the cylinder blocks had been made from cast iron, while the specially sand-cast crankcase components also added weight, so there was obviously plenty of potential. One clever feature of the design, even if it looked like production expediency, was the way in which

The crankcase (below) consists of separate castings bolted together, requiring care in assembly. Three exhausts lead into two pipes, terminating in the extraordinary 'ray gun' silencers with three short exit pipes.

Science-fiction styling and superbike performance were the two main attributes of the 1968 BSA Rocket 3, designed to appeal to a largely American market.

BSA Rocket 3 (1968)

Years in production: BSA Rocket 3 1968-72

Engine type: three-cylinder ohv four-stroke

Bore and stroke: 67 x 70mm

Capacity: 740cc

Compression ratio: 9.5:1

Power: 60bhp @ 7250rpm

Gearbox: four-speed in unit

Tyres (front/rear): $3\frac{1}{4}$ x 19in/ 4 x 19in

Wheelbase: 57in

Weight: 490lb

Top speed: 120mph

the crankshaft was made. To give even firing, this had to have three throws at 120 degrees to each other – a complicated forging. So instead, the shaft was forged•in one plane, then heated and twisted to the correct angles. Inevitably, part of the heritage of the engine design was that it was both costly and complicated to manufacture. Two versions – a BSA and a Triumph – were actually developed, using a different engine and frame layout, with the BSA's engine angled forward in a duplex cradle frame. The crankcase was a bolt-up assembly of five major castings in place of the two used by most of the competition, and indeed, the original Triumph twins. Care in component selection and engine building were essential.

Production of the first Rocket 3, as BSA were to call their version of the triple, began in 1968, and the machine was launched in Britain early in 1969 – slightly ahead of

Honda's revolutionary 750 four – to mixed reactions. Road tests showed that it was the fastest multi-cylinder production machine of the era, and although it was slightly slower to accelerate than either the Norton Commando or the Honda, it had the legs of both at the top end. In 1971 a Rocket 3 won the Daytona 200 in the United States, with a new race record speed, while a Trident placed second and another BSA placed third.

The styling was far less well-received. Designed by committee, and in response to the demands of the huge American market, the Rocket 3's slab-sided petrol tank, huge badges and 'ray gun' silencers were not what the traditional BSA buyer expected. Only about 7000 were built before financial difficulties meant production shut down in 1972, leaving the Triumph Trident to inherit the mantle of the triples.

Triumph T120 Bonneville

Triumph's Speed Twin had been one of the bikes that helped to set the pace before the war. After the conflict, the 500cc Speed Twin spawned many descendants, from 350 to 750cc capacity. Above all others, the 650cc Bonneville became the bike that set the standard throughout the late 1950s and 1960s – the era of the Rockers and Café Racers.

The first 650cc Triumph appeared in 1949, when the softly tuned 6T Thunderbird showed its pace at the Monthléry speed bowl before going on sale the next year. The model was an excellent tourer, marred only by two failings – the increased level of vibration that had caused one of the Monthléry entries to record a slower time than it should have, and the crude rear suspension offered by Triumph's sprung hub.

Even so, a Thunderbird racer, equipped with twin carburettors, hot cams and high-compression pistons, managed to better 132mph at Utah's Bonneville Salt Flats in 1951. A few years later, in 1956, Johnny Allen made a world speed record bid in a streamlined shell fitted with two 6T engines. Although he achieved 214.4mph, a record accepted by the US authorities, the world governing body refused to acknowledge it. Undaunted, American enthusiasts continued their efforts, and two years later a specially prepared Tiger 110 (a 650 with rear swing arm and hotter engine than the Thunderbird) managed to achieve over 147mph, ridden by Bill Johnson. The speed was good enough for a class record. That was in 1958, and the venue once again was Bonneville.

The first Triumph machine to bear the Bonneville name appeared in 1959. Based heavily on the Tiger 110, the T120 was fitted with the twin carburettors that were optional on the T110, together with the hot E3134 inlet cam. With a power rated at 46 bhp, the model was already good for a comfortable 115mph – perhaps more – but the engine had the potential to be tuned a lot hotter.

The first Bonnevilles could easily outperform the handling of their cycle parts, but from 1963 onwards they

Light and sporty, Triumph's 650 twin had an edge over its more staid competitors, which made it the machine that a generation aspired to. Although its general layout harked back some 30 years, it had been revised year-on-year, giving an unrivalled blend of power and handling.

Front braking (left) is by a twin-leading-shoe 8in diameter drum that stopped the light (370lb) package reasonably effectively.

gained a new frame, with extra bracing for the swinging arm and steering head. At the same time, the separate engine and gearbox became part of a new unitary design. As a result the power unit became more compact, and now contributed to the stiffness of the package. A couple of years later, the steering angle was changed and improved forks adopted.

All these improvements helped Triumph's Bonneville to match the all-round performance available from its rivals. In the styling stakes, however, it had no equal. Where the contemporary BSA was worthy but perhaps a little stolid, and Norton's offering lacked the absolute glamour of its racing forebears, the 650 Bonneville oozed get-up-and-go.

On the race track, it got up and went. In 1967 and 1969 it won Production TTs and British 500 mile races. The works T100R gave 55 bhp and was timed at over 140mph in the

TT. In 1969 it achieved a 1/2/3 in the Thruxton 500-miler, covering three more of the top seven places.

Bonnevilles attract strong supporters, and several different years have their proponents. In the opinion of many, however, the 1968 is the best of the breed. With good handling and more reliable electrics than its predecessors (including a new ignition system), all the good features were there in a package that was hard to beat. But it was almost the end of the line, for the 650 twin would survive a scant three years before it was replaced by a new 750 and Triumph began its slow slide into oblivion.

Triumph T120 Bonneville (1968)

Years in production: 1959-71

Engine type: twin-cylinder ohv four-stroke

Bore and stroke: 71 x 82mm

Capacity: 649cc

Compression ratio: 8.5:1

Power: 46bhp @ 6700rpm

Carburation: two $1\frac{3}{16}$in Amal Monoblocs

Gearbox: four-speed

Wheelbase: 55in

Weight: 370lb

Norton Commando (Fastback)

Launched to rapturous acclaim at the Earls Court Show in 1967, and four times voted Machine of the Year, the Norton Commando was perhaps the best loved product of the final years of the British industry. And yet it grew from a classic compromise. By the mid-60s, Associated Motorcycles (AMC), the parent company of the AJS, Matchless and Norton concerns – among many other great names of the British industry – was in trouble. In late 1966 the firm was taken over by Manganese Bronze Holdings, an engineering conglomerate which already owned Villiers. Under the chairmanship of Dennis Poore, the head of MBH and a one-time racing driver, the motorcycle interests were merged into Norton Villiers.

Prior to this production had consisted of a range of variations of AJS's, Matchless' and Norton's old twins and singles, many of which had been dropped as poor sellers after 1962. Virtually all the current product consisted of 650 and 750cc Norton twins, using either the ageing Featherbed or Matchless frame. It was clear that the new company needed a flagship – and quickly, preferably by the next year's show. Efforts initially centred on an existing design that had been underway some years before. Called the P10, this was a double overhead-camshaft parallel twin, but after several months development it was apparent that the machine would prove too heavy, too rough and potentially too unreliable.

With only some three months to go before the show, development engineers Bernard Hooper and Bob Trigg, together with engineering director Dr Stefan Bauer, suggested an alternative. Bauer had joined Norton Villiers in January 1967 from Rolls Royce. Not a motorcyclist, he argued that conventional frame design was contrary to good engineering principles, and suggested that the P10 should have a frame based on a single top tube. Bauer also insisted that engine vibration could not be tolerated – and it was vibration that was one of the chief complaints with the existing Norton twins.

Developed from the 497cc Dominator of the early 1950s, the twins had grown through 596 and 646cc, and finally to the 745cc unit used in the Featherbed-framed Atlas, gaining power at the expense of a little more roughness each time. The idea that was now put forward was completely radical – why not fit a modified version of the tried-and-tested

This model, one of the first ten made, is finished in conventional Norton silver with red and black striping, a far cry from the colourful show machine.

Norton Commando Fastback (1967)

Years in production: 1967-73

Engine type: parallel twin ohv four-stroke

Bore and stroke: 73 x 89 mm

Capacity: 745cc

Compression ratio: 8.9:1

Power: 58bhp @ 6500rpm

Carburettors: Amal concentric

Tyres (front/rear): 3 x 19in/ $3\frac{1}{2}$ x 19in

Wheelbase: $56\frac{3}{4}$ in

Top speed: 120mph

Atlas engine to a new frame based on Bauer's ideas? And to eliminate the problem of vibration, simply isolate the engine from the rider, together with the entire transmission train, including the rear wheel.

This was done by bolting the separate engine, gearbox and swinging-arm assembly together as one unit. The unit was then suspended from a spine frame based on a $2\frac{1}{4}$ in diameter top tube, using adjustable rubber bushes at three carefully calculated points. The idea worked superbly, allowing the engine to shake to its heart's content without disturbing the rider, and in 1969 the idea won an award for the most significant contribution to motorcycling. Inclined slightly forward, the modified Atlas engine had an aggressive stance and possessed enormous grunt.

Styling on the prototype was carried out by design consultants Wolf Ohlins, another company with no motorcycling experience. It included a silver frame and tank, and an orange seat with curious 'ears' projecting forward to hug the tank. Ar the rear it featured a racy hump, which led to the model being dubbed the 'Fastback'. Much lighter than its predecessors, the machine went as well as it looked. Acceleration was phenomenal for its day, under five seconds to reach 60mph, leading to a top speed of nearly 120mph.

Fastback styling took the motorcycle world by storm in 1967. A forward angled engine, fibreglass seat tail, and 'ears' coming forward from the seat to embrace the tank all hinted at the 120mph performance of which the machine was capable.

Norton P11

Norton's P11 'desert sled' was one of the British industry's inspired compromises. Something of a 'parts-bin special' it was a mix-and-match combination of parts from Norton and parent company AMC, designed to suit the American market and originally for export only. The result was so good that although few found their way on to British roads, those that did, along with many more recent re-imports, rapidly achieved cult status. With the enormous popularity of powerful, off-road twins that began in the 1980s, it can now also be seen as a machine that was way ahead of its time.

The P11 predated Norton's more famous Commando, but in many ways it shared similar reasons for its existence. The firm's Dominator twins had been developed to the limit while – despite the pedigree of its Featherbed frame – their 750cc derivative the Atlas was starting to look its age. With cutbacks becoming a necessity in the mid 1960s, AMC was keen to reduce the model variations and dispose of stock.

America still formed a big part of the market, where leisure motorcycling was far more significant than in Britain. Off-road sport in particular had long been an important sales area, and it was this that led to the launch of the P11. AMC's US distributor suggested that it might be possible to construct a machine especially for the popular West Coast desert races. AMC's Matchless G85CS had satisfied just such a market. Essentially a racing 500cc engine in a

Conceived as a racer first and foremost, in the late 1960s Norton's 'desert sled' took first place in California's Mojave desert for two years running. The powerful, lightweight package that resulted became a cult roadster.

lightweight scrambler frame, it had been very successful, but was now outclassed on power. In 1965 Norton had tried a version of the Atlas – the Scrambler – but it was far too heavy to be competitive.

And so the P11 was born. It used the Atlas engine as modified for the scrambler. But in place of the heavy roadster-based cycle parts, the frame was the lightweight unit of the Matchless. Lightness was the key, for together with the powerful Atlas engine it provided a brutal power-to-weight ratio. The tank was as small as practicable and made of alloy. Mudguards, silencer, side panels and other fittings followed suit. Everything was built for one purpose only – winning. Win it did. In its intended home of the Mojave desert, the lightweight, powerful P11 reigned supreme through the closing years of the 1960s. That same power could get out of hand on the road, where with off-road tyres and a short wheelbase its handling was not always as sure as expected from a Norton.

Any criticism of its road performance missed the point, for no scrambler was equipped to deal with a performance of well over 100 mph on the tarmac. Lightweight, lean and purposeful, these machines were costly to build, because the Norton engine was a tight fit in the Matchless frame and needed special spacers to match up. Their schizophrenic existence was obvious from the fact that a near-identical model was marketed as the Matchless N15CS. But whatever their identity, the package worked superbly well, while their cut-down styling helped to define the street scrambler concept that would influence a whole generation of future roadsters. When both models were discontinued in 1969, they had already become a legend.

Norton P11 (1969)

Years in production: 1967-69

Engine type: 360 degree parallel twin ohv four-stroke

Bore and stroke: 73 x 89 mm

Capacity: 745cc

Compression ratio: 7.5:1

Power: 50bhp @ 6rpm

Carburettors: twin Amal Concentrics

Weight: 380lb

Top speed: 110mph

Norton Commando (Roadster)

The Norton Commando was well placed to exploit the dawning of the superbike era and it enjoyed a healthy level of sales right from the start. In 1969 a MkII version was introduced, along with the Commando S model, which had high-level exhausts, both running down the left of the machine, and the more conventionally styled Roadster.

The Commando was launched into competition right from the start, and it was not long before the 750 gained its first track success. It would go on to win a host of events and records, while the entry in the Production TT of 1970 narrowly missed a 100mph lap.

The 750 models continued until late 1973, with various styling and mechanical changes. These variants included the bizarre Hi-Rider, which had extreme Chopper styling featuring ultra high-rise bars and a seat with an extended backrest. But there was also a change that spelled near disaster. This was the introduction of the Combat engine in 1972, a year that also saw the use of a front disc brake for the first time.

The Combat engine was developed with the idea of improving the power and performance. It had a strengthened bottom end, hot cams, high compression and gas-flowed head. Although this seemed like a good idea, it was almost fatal for the model. The over-stressed main bearings frequently gave way after as few as 5000 miles, while oil leaks and damage from over-revving were depressingly common. Retrospectively, the problems were cured by fitting a new type of main bearing and lowering the compression ratio, but the Combat engine had been an expensive folly.

It was a pity that the record of the 750 had been tarnished in this way, for the potential of the design was well demonstrated by some spectacular success on the race track. Following his success in production racing with the early 750, Norton's brilliant rider-developer Peter Williams set out to see just what could be done to make the bike competitive in Formula 750. Sponsored by the John Player tobacco company, his development led to a

model with a monocoque version of an isolastic frame, which doubled as the fuel tank, and a tailored fairing that directed air to the engine and carburettors. Highly efficient, the fairing made up for a massive power deficiency against the opposition. After a run of frustration and disappointment, Williams came home in the 1973 Formula 750 TT to a famous win, with the fastest lap of 107.57mph. His team-mate Mick Grant was second.

The 750cc models were phased out in October 1973, by which time they were designated MkV models, and with the problems cured, were as attractive in their way as the original Fastback 750s had been.

The MkI 850cc replacements had appeared earlier that year, and would remain in production through three mark changes until 1975. By that time they had gained (rather ineffective) electric starting and numerous modifications, all aimed at helping the Commando to compete with the reliability and performance of its competition – chiefly the new generation of Japanese superbikes.

Sadly, by this time the parent company's financial difficulties and the problems of manufacture on worn, old machinery made it increasingly difficult to compete. While the machines were rightly loved by a generation of owners, it had to be acknowledged that running a Commando required a level of dedication and sympathy far higher than that demanded by a Honda or Kawasaki. And for Norton it would prove impossible to compete in selling what was effectively one design to a tiny proportion of the market. Despite its proud heritage and enviable record, the Commando succumbed to old age and market pressures, with a final trickle of machines in 1978. Although the Norton name would live on in the form of the rotary-engined machines built at Shenstone in Staffordshire, the Commando marked the end of a line that had begun a long way back in the pioneer era.

Norton Commando Roadster (1973)

Years in production: 1967-73 (750) 1973-78 (850)

Engine type: parallel twin ohv four-stroke

Bore and stroke: 73 x 89mm (750) 77 x 89mm (850)

Capacity: 745cc (750) 829cc (850)

Compression ratio: 9:1 (750) 10:1 (Combat) 8.5:1 (850)

Power: 60bhp (750) 68bhp (Combat) 60bhp @ 6000rpm (850) (claimed)

Carburettors: 30mm Amal Concentrics 32mm (Combat and 850)

Tyres (front/rear): 4.10x19

Top speed: 125mph (claimed)

Like the other later variants of the Commando, the Roadster was conventionally styled compared to its predecessors. Refinements included flashing indicators and a front disc brake. The disastrous 'improvement' of the over-tuned Combat engine used on other models was abandoned in 1973, the year of this 750cc MkV model.

Triumph Trident

The story of the Triumph Trident began as part of the same development process that had spawned the BSA Rocket 3. But where the BSA soon went out of production, it was the Triumph that really proved the concept.

The first version of the Trident had an upright engine in a frame based on the single downtube Bonneville, quite unlike the BSA's angled engine and duplex frame, which meant that most of the major castings were completely different. By contrast to the BSA's radical styling, which had helped to contribute to its poor sales, Triumph's version, the T150 Trident, had a family likeness to the contemporary twin, especially after a redesign in 1972.

Whatever the reason, the Trident sold much better than the Rocket 3, and about 45,000 were made. This was despite weaknesses in quality control, as a result of which oil leaks and electrical faults were distressingly common. The drum brakes initially used were weak for a machine with such high performance, and had to be modified, although

The T150 version of the Trident (above) has an upright engine, like the upright Triumph twin on which it was based. The frame has a single downtube similar to the twin's, and unlike the BSA version of the triples.

discs were fitted to later models. The engine, too, needed heavy maintenance over a lengthy running-in period. Fortunately the unconventional crank, produced by twisting a straight forging, eventually proved strong enough to last throughout the model's production life and to cope with uprated power outputs of around 100bhp.

There was a much happier story in competition, as the triples proved competitive right from the start; although they were not without a few problems. One Trident racer acquired legendary status after a massive oil leak at the 1970 Bol d'Or, which led to it acquiring lurid handling and

Triumph Trident T160 (1974)

Years in production: 1969-1974 (T150)
　　　　　　　　　　　　1974 (T160)

Engine type: three-cylinder ohv four-stroke

Bore and stroke: 67 x 70mm

Capacity: 740cc

Compression ratio: 9.5:1

Power: 58bhp @ 7250rpm

Gearbox: four-speed in unit

Tyres (front/rear): 4.10 x 19in/4.10 x 19in

Wheelbase: 58in

Weight: 525lb

Top speed: 115mph

the nickname 'Slippery Sam'. Even so, triples won most of the important short-circuit competitions, as well as taking the first three places in the 1971 Production TT.

In Rocket 3 form, the triples' styling had already veered to the flamboyant, but in 1972 it was taken to excess with a model styled by the young American designer Craig Vetter. Planned as a limited-edition model to appeal to American tastes, it was called the X75 Hurricane, and blended elements of a stripped flat-track racer with the chopper styling brought into vogue by the recent film *Easy Rider*. Considered outrageous at the time, in hindsight it can be seen to have had an enormous effect on motorcycle styling.

From 1974 Triumph offered a new and much more conventional triple, the T160, using a version of the BSA's inclined engine, with, for the first time, an electric start to augment the kick-starter.

A number of variants of this model found their way on to the British market as the Cardinal. They were in fact part of a batch that had been destined for police use in the Middle East, but redirected when the deal fell through. This was effectively the end of the design. There had been plans to launch a 900cc version, as well as a 1000cc four, but this was not to be, and with the imminent financial collapse of the parent company, Triumph was forced to concentrate on the much simpler twins.

The final version of the Trident owed a great deal to the BSA Rocket 3, from which it borrowed the inclined engine. But unlike the heavy, over-styled BSA, the T160 was a lithe machine in the mould of previous generations of Triumph twins.

Rickman Enfield Interceptor

The Rickman Interceptor mated one of the biggest engines produced by the British industry to one of the best frames. Much lighter than its forebears, it had better handling and one of the first really effective disc brakes. It should have been a splendid success, but in reality it represented a glorious swan song for one of the industry's great pioneers.

By the late 1960s the Rickman brothers Don and Derek were firmly established as makers of high-quality frames for sports machines, off-roaders and even police bikes. Over the years they would produce packages for the popular Japanese engines, then diversify into accessories and kit car manufacture.

As Rickman began their rise, so Royal Enfield began to sink. Their flagship, the 750 Interceptor, had been launched in 1963, but while it was a promising new model the company was already in the same kind of financial trouble that had gripped much of the industry.

The company's new owners had launched an ambitious programme of new models and had thrown themselves enthusiastically into racing, but further cutbacks proved necessary, and the old Redditch works was closed in 1966. Engines and other parts were now built in a new factory, while the once-popular 250 singles ceased manufacture, and production of Interceptor frames was farmed out to Velocette. The company changed hands again in 1967, becoming part of the Norton Villiers group. Velocette now took over the spares operation, which they ran until they themselves closed in 1971.

Interceptors continued to be made throughout this period, although there was a gap between 1965 and 1967, when the model reappeared as the Series 1A. In 1968 the Series II model was launched. Substantially different from the earlier machines, these had a Norton front end, redesigned engine, clutch and ignition. Powerful and generally reliable, they were offered in an American styling with high bars that made hard work of the high top speeds possible, while the outmoded gearbox was awkward to use.

Around 1000 engines had been made when Royal Enfield abruptly ceased trading, leaving these power units surplus to requirements. Several hundred were bought by the American Floyd Clymer, a publisher who had recently aquired the Indian name, intending to relaunch the marque. The Indian Enfield 750 was sold in America from 1969.

The remaining batch went to Rickman, who built a short run using their nickel-plated duplex frame with their own design of front fork, 10in disc brakes and fibreglass body parts. Styling was an odd mix of café racer and tourer with high-rise bars clamped to the fork stanchions. Despite their quality and an excellent performance, the bikes were hampered by a high price as well as reservations about the engine and, particularly, the gearbox. Sales were slow, and under 140 were built in two years. Despite that, their charm and rarity ensured that they rate as one of the true classics from the declining British industry, while the survival of the Enfield name was a timely reminder of a firm that had helped to bring about its birth.

Rickman Enfield Interceptor (1974)

Years in production: 1970-2 (some registered later)

Engine type: 360 degree parallel twin ohv four-stroke

Bore and stroke: 71 x 93mm

Capacity: 636cc

Compression ratio: 8.5:1

Power: 56bhp @ 6750rpm

Carburettors: twin Amal Concentrics

Tyres (front/rear): $4\frac{1}{8}$ x 18in/$4\frac{1}{8}$ x 18in

Weight: 365lb

Top speed: 120mph

Stylish and purposeful, the Rickman frame package included their own frame, forks and pioneering disc brakes, as well as fibreglass tank and bodywork. Refinished in red, the result is far more effective than the original models, which were finished in blue apart from side panels in white – seemingly an incomplete afterthought. One of the last batch made, this model was not registered until 1974.

Silk 700

In the mid 1970s the Silk gained a reputation for being one of the best-handling machines of the day – although its reliability and outright speed never attracted quite the same eulogies. It might have been unfair to expect any more, for the Silk, built by a small specialist engineering company based in Derbyshire, was a direct descendant of the venerable Scott two-stroke.

Company founder George Silk was a precision engineer who had trained with an ex-Scott employee and restorer, while his own father was active in the owners' club. He himself rode and tuned vintage Scotts in the 1960s, and when, at the end of the decade, he set up in business as a specialist engineer, Silk Engineering offered a repair and parts service for Scotts as a sideline. The services included a number of modifications aimed at providing increased reliability and power, improving both the bottom end, the lubrication and the gas flow.

The chief improvement, however, lay in a frame that offered modern technology in a concept much closer to Alfred Scott's original ideas than anything produced in the previous 30 years. The frame was a product of nearby Spondon Engineering, a relative newcomer to the world of specialist frame-building for racers. Spondon's frames for Japanese racing two-strokes were light, stiff and well triangulated, with modern suspension at both ends. They made their own forks and

Recognisably a derivative of the 70-year-old Scott design, Silk's water-cooled two-stroke twin was far from being outclassed in the technology stakes by the Japanese competition. But the lack of investment required for true volume production meant that it was ultimately doomed to remain a specialist item.

brakes, too – and the whole package could easily be adapted to the engines that Silk was building.

The radiator was either a Scott-type or borrowed from an LE Velocette, and the final piece in this most British of jigsaws was the gearbox – based on the late Velocette four-speed design, modified to allow it to be a built in unit with the engine. The 20 Scott-based Silk Specials constructed by 1975 were just that – specials built as a blend of disparate components.

With assistance from some of Britain's foremost engineering specialists the Scott-based engine was substantially redesigned, with a patented scavenging system backed up by specially developed silencers, resulting in a smooth, powerful engine with good fuel economy. Other modern features, such as state-of-the-art electronic ignition, were designed in from the start.

> ## Silk 700 (1978)
>
> *Years in production:* 1975-79
>
> *Engine type:* twin-cylinder water-cooled two-stroke
>
> *Bore and stroke:* 76 x 72mm
>
> *Capacity:* 653cc
>
> *Compression ratio:* 8 5:1 (MkII)
>
> *Power:* 54bhp @ 6000rpm (MkII)
>
> *Gearbox:* four-speed
>
> *Weight:* 309lb

The result of all this work was the Silk 700S – clearly derived from the previous Specials, but a proper production machine with parts manufactured by Silk or its suppliers. Although clearly a limited volume, hand built machine, it bristled with clever ideas and practical features such as rear chain enclosure. In a time when superbikes were becoming heavier and heavier, the most attractive feature of the 700S was its very absence of weight – less than many Japanese lightweights for the power output of a middleweight. Together with the excellent Spondon frame, this contributed to the superb handling and good acceleration.

Producing such a machine in small numbers was fraught with difficulties – not least financial – and Silk found the going hard at a time when most of the British industry was collapsing. There was no way in which the Silk could have attracted a mass market or financed volume production. Fewer than 150 were built.

Triumph T140 Bonneville

The Triumph Bonneville was nothing if not a survivor. Clearly based on Edward Turner's prewar concept, it continued to uphold the traditional values of the company while trying to adopt the modern conveniences that a new generation of riders demanded. And despite a number of obvious shortcomings, it continued to win friends and admirers throughout the superbike era.

The last of the long line of Triumph twins had an inauspicious beginning, when its launch was delayed by a whole series of design problems. It began in 650cc form when the current Bonneville engine gained a new frame in 1971. It was heavily based on the frame used for the BSA A65, sharing its oil-in-frame design, and had similar shortcomings as a result of an excessively high seat. There were also numerous teething troubles, but the bike was reasonably well received.

A year later the frame was lowered and there were a number of detail changes, including the introduction of a five-speed gearbox option. By now, 'mod-cons' such as indicators were the norm, but with its drum brakes and kick-start, the T120 Bonneville was years behind such competitors as the Honda 750 Four launched three years earlier. Vibration and oil consumption were also a problem, but the handling continued to set a standard that the Japanese competition could not match.

The first 750cc versions appeared the following year as the T140V. Essentially, this was a bored-out 650 and, apart from minor variations, it shared the smaller bike's cycle parts, which now included a new front disc brake. The first few models

were 724cc, but this soon settled at 744cc with a slightly larger bore. More softly tuned than the 650, the engine was also strengthened, with more positive location for the head and an extra holding-down stud; the transmission was beefed up, and there were other detail changes.

The parallel twin's vibration was worse on the new model, and it was slow to gain acceptance, especially while the 650cc ran alongside it. Worse still, the Meriden factory's problems reached a head late in 1973, ultimately resulting in the workers' occupation. No new machines appeared until mid 1974, and those that did emerge showed evidence of hasty finishing. The following year matters improved as the workers' cooperative got underway and settled down to doing what they knew best. Existing machines were sold off to make way for a new model, with an engine that had been modified to suit the American market's insistence on a left-foot gearchange – a regulation that was introduced in 1974.

Triumph T140 Bonneville (1978)

Years in production: 1973-88

Engine type: twin-cylinder ohv four-stroke

Bore and stroke: 76 x 82mm

Capacity: 744cc

Compression ratio: 7.9:1

Power: 49bhp @ 6500rpm

Carburation: Two 30mm Amal Concentrics

Gearbox: five-speed

Tyres front/rear: $4\frac{1}{8}$ x 19in/$4\frac{1}{8}$ x 18in

Wheelbase: 55in

Weight: 395lb

Top speed: 111mph

Quality control proved a problem with antiquated machinery and limited funds, but by 1977 the factory was able to offer a limited-edition Jubilee model, to mark the Queen's Silver Jubilee. With a number of minor refinements introduced in 1978, the T140, as the model was now styled, had become a reasonably sound, if anachronistic, option.

The year 1979 brought the launch of the T140E – which had a new cylinder head and carburettors aimed at meeting new American emission laws – and the T140D, a custom special. Around 20,000 machines based on the new design were built before Triumph finally went to the

wall. These included an 'executive' tourer, latterly including the first electric start model, an economy 650 version, a trail variant and finally the eight-valve TSS and custom TSX.

The Meriden cooperative went into liquidation in 1982. The assets were bought by John Bloor, although he assigned limited rights to build the Bonneville to Les Harris's Devon-based company. Harris built a limited number of Bonnies between 1985 and 1988, but although this spelt the end for the old twin, by then Bloor's own plans to write a new chapter in the Triumph story were well-advanced.

Old world charm for the new world: American specification features include high bars and traditional streamlined Triumph tank. The simple controls and instruments show little concession to the ergonomics which were starting to dominate design thinking in the 1970s – although they are efficient enough to operate for all that.

The traditional virtues of Triumph's 750cc twin included light weight, simplicity and good handling. But there were few concessions to the contemporary world of superbikes, with the exception of a front disc brake and flashing indicators. The engine was clearly heavily in debt to the 40-year-old Speed Twin, with 'modernisations' such as the left-foot, five-speed gearchange very much an afterthought.

Hesketh Vampire

By the late 1970s it was obvious to all that the British industry had been in terminal decline for a long time. So when it leaked out that someone was preparing to invest substantially in a completely new model, it was greeted with enthusiasm from many sides. If, for all its good points, the motorcycle that they got failed to live up to its promise, it came to be seen as just another symptom of the British malaise.

The man behind the machine was colourful character Lord Hesketh, a fully fledged baron with a substantial inheritance, which included an impressive estate in Northamptonshire. In 1973 Hesketh, then aged just 22, had run a Formula One car-racing team with impressive results, and in 1975 came fourth in the World Championship.

Financially, however, things were not going so well and in 1974 Hesketh decided to supplement his company's racing car engineering work by developing a motorcycle

Hesketh Vampire (1984)

Years in production: 1982-83

Engine type: four-valve 90 degree V-twin four-stroke

Bore and stroke: 95 x 70 mm

Capacity: 992cc

Compression ratio: 10.5:1

Carburettors: 36mm Amal MkII Concentric/Dell'Orto PHFs

Wheelbase: 59½in

Weight: 506lb (V1000) 544lb (Vampire)

Top speed: 120mph

Impressive instrumentation (right) included a clock and a gauge to show the ambient temperature. Hydraulic operation for the clutch was a Hesketh innovation.

that could capitalise on both their racing record and the kind of British handmade exclusivity that went with his lordship's name.

Several ideas were floated, including buying the near-defunct Norton factory or making frame kits for Japanese bikes. But motorcycle sales were enjoying a boom and outside the Japanese four-cylinder conformity, European twins were growing in popularity. In 1977 Hesketh began talks with engine specialists Weslake that would result in the development of the company's own 1000cc V-twin – a classically British type of engine that was proving to be a great success for Ducati.

Unfortunately the project soon ran into trouble, while behind the scenes finance was proving difficult. Many of the troubles centred on the conflicting demands of Hesketh's largely car-based team of designers with Weslake's own engineers. The engine was heavily based on Weslake's successful four-valve singles, widely used in speedway.

Heavy and tall, the Vampire was a last-ditch attempt to make a success out of the failed Hesketh V1000 by turning it into a tourer. But the fairing offered inadequate protection, and the bike still suffered from the basic engineering deficiencies caused by a lack of development. Few sold, and the company foundered for a second time in the early 1980s.

But restrictions on the design meant there had to be many compromises, particularly in the layout of the gearbox.

Although problems began surfacing fairly early on, an enthusiastic press launch went ahead in the spring of 1980. The bike that went on show was traditionally styled, with a small cockpit fairing and handsomely plated frame. Its layout was similar to the contemporary Ducati 90 degree 'L-twin', although its chunky looks were a world away from the lithe Italian. At over 500 lb, the chunky looks were backed up by the facts.

As no existing factory was able to take on quantity manufacture, Hesketh set up his own at Daventry. Experienced staff were hired, and the process of putting the V1000 into production began.

In 1981 the first went on press test, with the result that criticism of the clunky gearchange, engine noise, handling and price became public. Urgent revisions were put in hand, but it became clear that Hesketh was short of money. When the bikes went on sale in February 1982 it was a matter of too little, too late. Only 100 or so were sold before the company was wound up in August 1982.

The postscript was not long in following. Hesketh and partners had formed a new firm, whose small team would sell a package of modifications for the existing machines, at the same time developing a new fully-faired tourer, the Vampire. But the gearbox faults, which included a host of false neutrals, persisted, while the engine was noisy and the fairing restricted the turning circle without giving adequate protection. After a couple of years only a handful had been sold, and there were further lay-offs. While members of the enthusiastic team continued their own development work, it was the end for Hesketh himself and yet another last hope for the British industry.

The unfaired V1000 (left): the massive Hesketh engine – the cause of most of the troubles – was slung from a simple, plated tube frame. Problems included oil leaks from the chaincases to the overhead-camshafts, heavy vibration and a lumpy gearchange, despite a low state of tune.

Norton Wankel Rotary

Although it ended up wearing a Norton badge, the British rotary spent years being batted about between the various company groups that formed as the industry went into terminal decline. When it finally appeared, years after the concept first saw metal, some viewed it as little short of a miracle, while others were sceptical about the long-term potential of an engine type that was already being seen as something of a lost cause.

When Norton rotaries started to win races, some were overjoyed, while others enjoyed wrangling about the technicalities of the engine classification and whether it was competing fairly. Whatever else, the Norton rotary was a brave effort by a small and dedicated team that added an important chapter to the story of the British motorcycle.

The Wankel engine was invented by Germany's Dr Felix Wankel, who took a first patent on the principle in the late 1920s. It was not until the late 1950s that a workable prototype was developed by Wankel, then working at NSU. The engine was used in some NSU cars, notably the Ro80, and showed so much promise that manufacturers worldwide rushed to buy licences to build them.

The Wankel's apparent advantages were numerous: doing away with the dozens of moving parts of a conventional piston engine, and replacing them with a simple rotor around which the normal cycle of induction, compression, ignition and exhaust were continually taking place, offering incredible smoothness. Unfortunately it was not that simple, with early problems arising as a result of the complexity of sealing and lubricating the rotor.

Rotary-engined machines appeared throughout the 1970s, including motorcycles from Suzuki, Hercules/DKW, Van Veen Kriedler and a prototype Yamaha. Only the Suzuki RE5 was built in any quantity, and it proved too heavy and thirsty to become anything more than a curiosity. The only company to make much of a success of the concept was Mazda, notably with the RX7 sports car.

Among the experimenters was the BSA group, at that time a massive conglomerate with extensive R&D facilities.

The unconventional shape of Norton's air-cooled twin-rotor engine (above) harks back to a prototype developed by BSA as early as 1971. The concept originally developed by Dr Felix Wankel, working for NSU in Germany, offered smooth power with few moving parts. The practice was not so simple.

Using a proprietary German engine with a single rotor and fan cooling, an experimental machine was built in 1969. Having identified several problem areas, BSA built its own prototype in 1970, using an air-cooled twin-rotor layout, and a year later came up with an idea that greatly improved cooling efficiency.

As the decade wore on, BSA's increasing financial difficulties led to cutbacks that threatened the programme, but it was still alive as BSA was taken over by the Norton-Villiers-Triumph group. Prototypes were press tested in 1974, but a year later NVT collapsed.

The rotary project was salvaged from the collapse and given to a small but expert team based at Shenstone in Staffordshire. There they continued development on a tiny budget. Their work bore fruit in the early 1980s when several police forces and the armed forces took delivery of the Interpol II, with an engine clearly derived directly from the BSA prototype in a pressed-steel frame. The engine also found a new home as a power unit for ultralight aircraft.

There were several problems with the police bikes, although they showed obvious promise. It was not until 1987 that the company launched the limited edition unfaired Classic, designed to test the market. At the end of

Behind its fairing, the Commander concealed a liquid-cooled version of the twin-rotor engine developing 85 bhp, good enough to propel the tourer to around 125mph. The panniers were initially integral with the bodywork. The brakes, like the front wheel, were culled from the XJ900 Yamaha, and helped to slow a heavy machine that possessed minimal engine braking, like a two-stroke.

Norton Wankel Rotary (1987)

Years in production: 1987 (Classic)

Engine type: twin-rotor air-cooled rotary

Capacity: 588cc

Compression ratio: 7.5:1

Power: 79bhp @ 9000rpm

Carburettor: 1½in constant vacuum

Tyres (front/rear): 100/90 V18/ 120/80 V18

Wheelbase: 58½in

Weight: 498lb

Top speed: 120mph

Classic Norton: the unfaired silver machine with red and black coachlining was deliberately designed to recall traditional values. Based on the company's police bikes, the Classic was produced as a limited edition, complete with authentication certificate, as a means of testing the civilian market.

the year, the fully-equipped Commander, with a liquid-cooled version of the engine, was launched to many plaudits, despite its premium price and rather high fuel consumption.

A prototype racer was also under development, and when this finally took to the track it showed enormous potential, although there was a dispute as to whether its unconventional engine should be classified as a 588cc, as Norton claimed, or much more. Eventually the governing bodies settled on a formula that enabled it to compete as a 1000cc machine. By the end of the decade, with new sponsors JPS, the Nortons had won the British Formula One and Shell Supercup, and the Norton name was seen on a TT leaderboard for the first time since 1973.

From then on the Norton story became a bitter tale of dedicated engineers continuing to produce a trickle of

motorcycles, against a bewildering backdrop of corporate manoeuvring through a dire financial morass. But it may be premature to draw a line under the Norton story; after one hundred years in production, it is perhaps to be hoped that the firm may see its rebirth as a major force in the same way as Triumph.

Triumph Trident

The reborn, modern Triumph is a machine that can hold its head up with the best in the world. The marque that proved Britain could still produce a world-class motorcycle manufacturer after so many 'new British world-beaters' had foundered, Triumph has prospered by adopting the design traditions of the very Japanese machines that had helped to kill off the British bike. As far as most of the world was concerned, Triumph had come to an end with the collapse of the Meriden cooperative in 1981, although there had been an attempt to keep the Bonneville going beyond the death of the parent factory. But there were those who believed that the Triumph name still had something going for it – not least its thousands of devoted owners and enthusiasts. It was these people that the new owner of the Triumph name was counting on, when, out of the rubble of the old factory,

Triumph Trident (1995)

Engine type: liquid-cooled double overhead-cam in-line three-cylinder four-stroke

Bore and stroke: 76 x 65mm

Capacity: 885cc

Compression ratio: 10.6:1

Power: 98bhp @ 9000rpm

Carburettors: 3x36mm flat slide constant vacuum

Tyres (front/rear): 120/70 ZR17/ 180/55 ZR17

Wheelbase: 58½in

In its basic, unfaired touring form the Trident demonstrates the essence of the Hinckley Triumph concept. Recognisably modern and owing much to the Japanese tradition, the three-cylinder engine is in a class of its own, while the simple spine frame and suspension are adequate to the task without being over sophisticated.

a new company suddenly emerged at the end of the 1980s.

The owner was John Bloor. A large-scale property developer, he had amassed a considerable personal wealth by the time the old Triumph site was offered for sale. Together with the land, it turned out that the Triumph name and rights were also part of the package, a package that made Bloor the owner of the Triumph heritage.

What followed was a long period of secrecy, speculation and rumour. Finally, in 1988, the rumours were laid to rest when Bloor's company began building a new factory on a site at Hinckley, Leicestershire, where it was revealed a new range of Triumphs was to be built.

Secrecy still prevailed, however, perhaps because so much damage had been done to past revivals such as Hesketh and Norton by premature launches and too much speculation. The facts that did emerge made it clear that there was no connection other than name between Bloor's Triumph and the old Meriden company. Staff, machinery, designs and components were completely new.

The factory was completed in 1990 and the first machines were seen later that year at the German motorcycle show in Cologne – significantly the homeland of BMW rather than the old British industry, and an important international showcase. The first machine was the unfaired, touring Trident – its name and choice of three-cylinder engine being an important link with the old Triumph heritage. Production built up slowly but steadily from the first full year in 1992, with more models added on a gradual basis.

Triumph T595 Daytona

As the millenium approached, it was becoming clear what class of bike would rule the roost in the late 1990s. Sports bikes, as epitomised by Ducati's stylish 916 and Honda's hi-tech Fireblade, were the the machines that grabbed the headlines. For a new manufacturer like Triumph to compete at this level, a machine was needed that was both distinctively different and able to deliver the goods – no small undertaking for such a new company.

The solution was the T595 Daytona, which rapidly established itself as a bike with the capability to beat the best on the track as well as being a supremely usable street machine. Based on Triumph's trademark triple engine, it was in fact an all-new 955cc design with a double-overhead cam, and liquid-cooled power unit developed in association with the Lotus car race engineers. The object of the exercise was to optimise porting, valve and combustion chamber shapes, improving breathing. Stronger components ensured reliability at higher engine speeds and outputs, while new materials for non-stress-bearing components saved weight.

The engine management system, claimed to be the most complex and smartest ever fitted to a motorcycle, controlled the fuel injection and air induction, and could easily be adjusted to suit legislation in various markets, simply by replacing a tuning card. The full-power version gave 128bhp at 10,200rpm, with a massive 74 ft lb of torque peaking at 8,500rpm.

Matching the new engine was a new twin-spar perimeter frame that offered a radical departure from Triumph's successful spine concept, as well as an improvement on the competitors' offerings. Fabricated from aluminium extrusions and built-up sections, the frame used the engine as a stressed member to keep the weight down.

With a single-sided swinging arm and Japanese Showa suspension front and rear, handling was impeccable, while wheels, tyres and brakes were to the highest specification.

Versatility was one of the objectives of the design, which was aimed at providing the ultimate street bike as well as offering race-winning potential. The tucked-in silencer could easily be replaced with a full race component, while the sophisticated frame and forks were well up to the 160mph-plus potential of the stock machine.

Trumph also offered a stripped version of the same machine, the T509 Speed Triple, which allied a slightly lower performance to the fashionable 'street-fighter' look. Together, both machines demonstrated the technical capabilities of the new Triumph factory and showed that the British industry had fully shaken off its past problems to face a new era of motorcycling.

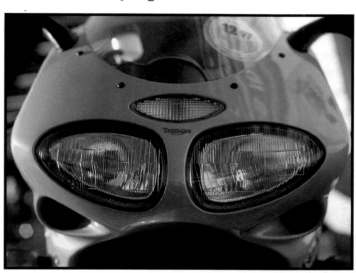

The slimline fairing with twin headlamps (above) offers the height of contemporary styling but conceals the hi-tech aluminium frame, the twin spars of which snake over the top of the three-cylinder power unit.

The distinctive three-spoke alloy wheels were designed by Triumph and produced in Italy aspecially for this model. The brakes, sourced in Japan, use four piston calipers with floating discs. The tucked-in silencer, designed to take advantage of the single-sided rear suspension, can be replaced with a racing unit.

Triumph T595 Daytona (1997)

Years in production: 1996—

Engine type: double overhead-cam four-stroke four-valve in-line triple

Capacity: 955cc

Bore and stroke: 79x65mm

Compression ratio: 11.2:1

Fuel system: Sagem fuel injection

Power: 128bhp @ 10,200rpm

Transmission: six-speed gearbox

Top speed: 161mph

Triumph Thunderbird

Although factory founder John Bloor had ridden a motorcycle in his youth, he was far from the mould of some of the many passionate enthusiasts who had tried to revive the British industry in the 1970s. As a hard-headed and successful businessman, he knew the value of brand loyalty and recognised the potential asset represented by such a well-respected name as Triumph.

Although the Triumph logo itself had been subtly redesigned, it was recognisably the same as the one that had graced the best-loved models in the company's history. Similarly, there were echoes of the old Triumph in the choice of a basic three-cylinder engine, and in the choice of the model names. With the average Hinckley Triumph buyer approaching 40 years of age, such historic resonances might be expected to strike a chord.

Triumph Thunderbird (1995)

Engine type: liquid-cooled double overhead-cam in-line three-cylinder four-stroke

Bore and stroke: 76 x 65mm

Capacity: 885cc

Compression ratio: 10.6:1

Power: 70bhp @ 8000rpm

Carburettors: 3 x 36mm flat slide constant vacuum

Tyres (front/rear): 110/80 18/160/80 16

Wheelbase: 58½in

With a tank, seat and mudguards which deliberately echo the styling of twins from Triumph's heyday, the Thunderbird proved an instant hit. The new model appealed to lovers of the British tradition while offering the sophistication that many new riders considered essential.

Nowhere was the sense of heritage stronger than with the new Thunderbird. Again, the model name was borrowed from the past, but this time, so was the styling. Happily for Triumph, a significant niche had opened in the market for machines that echoed the look and simplicity of older models, while offering the sophistication and reliability of new ones – an area that was already proving profitable for Japanese factories.

Triumph had a significant advantage in their choice of frame design. Although older in concept and inherently taller than the aluminum beam frames of contemporary fashion, the tubular spine frame was much simpler to construct or modify, while proving more than adequate to the task. Thus the Thunderbird acquired a tank and seat that were recognisably derived from the twins of the 1950s and 60s, old style mudguards and an engine that retained the modern features of the other models, including liquid-cooling – but was cleverly redesigned to look like its air-cooled forebears.

With power delivery to match the best of the competition, build quality intended to match BMW's and considerable development potential, Triumph's rebirth has almost single-handedly confounded the critics and proved that the British motorcycle has a future as well as a past. And with the 'retro' styling of its revived Thunderbird, Triumph has brought the British tradition full circle – even if, for some, it is a pastiche that flies in the face of everything the original stood for.

Manufacturers' badges from 1960 to present day